At a time of great personal trouble, and after having rejected the rigid religion of her childhood, Miriam Cameron returned *as an adult* to the Bible, looking for its verities, free of doctrinaire cant and dogma. This unique book is the outcome.

"I hope," says the author, "that this book can be useful to a wide variety of people: those who want an introduction to the Bible; young people who are trying to figure out what they believe; teachers who need help explaining concepts in the Bible to students; and the clergy who are always looking for new sermon ideas.

"Probably the people who will show the greatest interest in the book, however, are those who've rebelled against the religion, yet want a sense of spirituality and direction in life...I was that kind of person and I wrote the book for myself."

ATTENTION: SCHOOLS AND CORPORATIONS

WARNER books are available at quantity discounts with bulk purchase for educational, business, or sales promotional use. For information, please write to: SPECIAL SALES DEPARTMENT, WARNER BOOKS, 75 ROCKEFELLER PLAZA, NEW YORK, N.Y. 10019

**ARE THERE WARNER BOOKS
YOU WANT BUT CANNOT FIND IN YOUR LOCAL STORES?**

You can get any WARNER BOOKS title in print. Simply send title and retail price, plus 50¢ per order and 20¢ per copy to cover mailing and handling costs for each book desired. New York State and California residents add applicable sales tax. Enclose check or money order only, no cash please, to: WARNER BOOKS, P.O. BOX 690, NEW YORK, N.Y. 10019

"Hello, I'm God & I'm here to help you"

by Miriam Cameron

WARNER BOOKS

A Warner Communications Company

Thank you to
my family, the Millers, and Pamela Espeland

and to
Rev. Barry Carnine, Ron Curtis, Walt Fields,
Virginia Kivits, John LeDell, Ruth LeDell,
Rabbi Leigh D. Lerner, Michael Ormond,
Dr. Jonathan Paradise, Sandi Proehl,
Rev. James Roe, and Rabbi Barry I. Woolf.

WARNER BOOKS EDITION

Copyright © 1980 by Miriam E. Cameron
All rights reserved.

Cover photo by Springlife Studio

Book design by Helen Roberts

Warner Books, Inc., 75 Rockefeller Plaza, New York, N.Y. 10019

Ⓦ A Warner Communications Company

Printed in the United States of America

First Printing: June, 1980

10 9 8 7 6 5 4 3 2

Introduction

Hello, I'm God & I'm Here to Help You is a nonsexist, self-help book based on the Biblical teachings of Moses, the Prophets, and Jesus. It describes what the good life is and how to live it. It takes the often-complex principles of the Bible and states them in today's language without changing their original meaning. It discusses spiritual principles to live by without all the dogma of organized religion.

Since the book describes the principles many religions have in common rather than concentrating on their differences, it doesn't deal with doctrinal disputes. The book doesn't talk about Jesus by name, but people who believe that Jesus is God can easily substitute his name for God's. On the other hand, people who don't believe in a personal God at all can find the ideas helpful.

For simplicity, I wrote in the first person, as if God were speaking directly to the reader (the way the material is found in the Bible). Because of this, I didn't have to give God a sex as I would have if I'd written in the third person. This doesn't mean, however, that I think of God as a person; I don't. To me, God is the spiritual force in the world.

I used the English translations listed in the bibliography of the book, depending mainly upon *The Oxford Annotated Bible*, Revised Standard Version. Readers may want to compare the book with the Bible. That's why the Bible references used are listed at the end of the book. To show which are the appropriate references, numbers in the outer margin of the page of the text correspond with the numbers at the end of the book.

I hope this book can be useful to a wide variety of people: Those who want an introduction to the Bible; young people who are trying to figure out what they believe; teachers who need help explaining concepts in the Bible to students; and the clergy who are always looking for new sermon ideas.

Probably the people who will show the greatest interest in the book, however, are those who've rebelled against the religion of their childhood or against organized religion, yet want a sense of spirituality and direction in life. They've thrown out the baby with the bath water, want to get the baby back, and don't know how. This book tells them how in a way that's easy to understand. I know, because I was that kind of person, and I wrote the book for myself.

I grew up as the oldest child in an evangelical Lutheran minister's family. Although my father was officially the ordained minister, each of us felt responsible for "the lost." I spent much of my childhood helping my parents with their ministry in small Midwestern towns and traveling with them around this country, including Alaska, and in Canada on speaking engagements. My brother, three sisters, and I taught Sunday school and Bible school, played musical instruments, sang, and even gave sermons. At times, we took part in as many as five services on Sunday.

When I was a teenager, my father's religious beliefs began to change. After I had gone along with his new ideas for a while, I realized that I didn't want to conduct my life as he did his. This decision was hard for me because my father told me that if I rejected his viewpoints

I was rejecting God and that if I didn't obey God both my father and God would turn away from me. That meant the loss of my father's emotional, and also his financial, support.

After struggling with this problem for some time, I finally said to myself, "Who needs God? If God and religion are like my father, I don't want either one." But how would I conduct my life? I couldn't go back to the beliefs of my childhood. While majoring in nursing in college and later teaching the nursing of children, I learned the importance of having a philosophy that explains the goals of nursing practice and how to achieve them. I wished that I had time to develop a philosophy for my personal life, too. In the meantime, I'd try to be like "the norm."

I was accepted in graduate school, but my new husband put pressure on me to leave the city and move with him to his tiny hometown in order to manage his family's business. So instead of going to school, I went with my husband and stayed for six years.

Although there was enough money to buy a home and lakeside cabin and to travel extensively, these years were painful for me, mainly because I didn't know how to cope with the chemical dependency and related problems in the people around me. I hadn't yet started going to Al-Anon (an organization for families and friends of alcoholics) so I felt lonely and resentful. Out of desperation, I turned to what was familiar—Jesus' teachings. I wanted to discover for myself the "abundant life" Jesus talked about in the Bible.

I decided to take the time to write for myself a philosophy of life based on Jesus' teachings. After three years of study and writing, however, I concluded that I couldn't understand Jesus' teachings apart from the Old Testament, so I expanded my study to include it, too.

Gradually I came to the opinion that Moses, the Prophets, and Jesus all taught the same basic principles, so I combined them. I didn't try to solve such problems as how they had received their messages from God; whether their messages were, indeed, from God; whether they really taught what is attributed to them in the Bible; or whether there even is a God. I only wanted to describe in a personal philosophy of life what the Bible states these teachers said about the "good life," a term I substituted for the Biblical terms "abundant life" and "life."

First of all, I went through the Bible and wrote on separate pieces of paper every direct quotation from God and from Jesus, who claimed his message was from God. Next, I organized this volume of material according to pertinent subjects. Then I took one subject at a time and rewrote it so that I myself could easily understand it. I changed what I considered to be sexist terms: instead of "righteous man," I wrote "good person"; instead of "God our Father," I wrote "God our Parent."

Over the seven years that I worked on the book, many people asked for copies of it. Realizing that I couldn't afford to make a copy for everyone who asked for one, I rewrote the book with publication in mind. I offer it now with love in the hope that it will be as helpful to others as it has been to me.

Miriam Cameron

Contents

Introduction   v

I I WANT TO MAKE AN AGREEMENT WITH YOU   1
Who I am   1
I made the world good   3
Your responsibilities   4
You do it to yourself   6
It's your choice   7
You need to become a new person   8

II HOW TO BECOME A NEW PERSON   9
First, make things right with me   9
Next, make things right with other people   10
I forgive you   10
You're a new person   13
What happens if you turn away
  from me again?   14
What my guidelines are   16

III HOW TO LOVE ME   17
Remember that I'm the only true God   17
Love me completely   19

(ix)

Be my servant	20
Fight what's wrong	21
Pray to me	22
Keep the Sabbath	24
Don't be a hypocrite	24
Be humble	27
Don't try to buy the good life	28
Give me tithes and offerings	32
Take good care of the earth and its creatures	34
Take good care of yourself	35

IV HOW TO LOVE OTHER PEOPLE — 37
Love others as you love yourself	37
Be forgiving	38
Lend to people in need	40
Help those less fortunate than you	41
Do what's just	42
Tell the truth	43
Don't covet or steal	43
Don't murder	45
Choose leaders who keep my agreement	45
Be responsible in sexual relationships and in marriage	46
Care for your parents and children	47
Be kind to the people who work for you	48

V HOW TO TELL OTHER PEOPLE ABOUT ME — 50
Who my prophets were	50
Speak my words	51
Go to the world	52
What to say	54
Some people will accept you	55
Others will reject you	57

VI HOW TO COPE WITH TROUBLE — 61
Don't give in to temptation	61
Don't let false prophets influence you	63

Contents (xi)

Don't turn away from me if you're persecuted	67
Keep watch over yourself!	71

VII WHAT HAPPENS IF YOU BREAK MY AGREEMENT? — 76
Your thinking gets twisted	76
I reject you	80
You get confused and distressed	84
You're good for nothing	85
There's no hope for you	86

VIII WHAT HELL ON EARTH WOULD BE LIKE — 89
People reject me	89
People mistreat my followers	91
People aren't ashamed when they do wrong	
People choose bad leaders	93
Nations war against each other	95
Powerful nations rise and fall	97
The world is full of death	100
and destruction	101
The earth itself becomes an enemy	102
People get desperate	103
The world ends	105

IX WHAT THE GOOD LIFE IS LIKE — 106
I give you a new heart and my spirit	106
You and I have a special relationship	108
I answer your prayers	109
I take good care of you	110
I make you strong	112
I bless you	114
You're happy	115
You're good for the world	116
You live forever	118

X WHAT HEAVEN ON EARTH WOULD BE LIKE   120

People praise my followers   120
People turn to me   121
Troublemakers are stopped   124
Bad things have to go   125
People do what's good   128
The world is peaceful   130
The earth is fruitful again   131
Everyone is happy and prosperous   133

XI IT'S UP TO YOU!   135

Bible References   139
Bibliography   179

I
I WANT TO MAKE AN AGREEMENT WITH YOU

Are you unhappy? Maybe things seem all right on the surface, but underneath there's something wrong. Maybe nothing satisfies you anymore. You're anxious and confused. Sometimes you feel as if you've lost control of your own life. You don't know which way to turn.

I see what's happening to you, and I understand. I know you aren't living the good life. No matter how hard you try, you can't get on top of your problems all by yourself. I can, though, and I'm willing to help you.

Who am I and what can I do for you? I'll tell you about myself. 1

Who I am

Quite simply, I am God. 2
I'm the first and the last. I'm God of everyone who came before you and everyone who'll come after you. I've been here from the time of creation—and even before then—and I'll go on forever. 3

I'm one God, and I'm ruler of the universe. No god came before me, and no god will come after me. I'm the only true God—there's no one else like me.

I'm almighty; I can help or hurt. I never get weak or tired. All things are possible for me; there's nothing I can't do. I'm everywhere; I fill heaven and earth. No human being can do what I do or be what I am.

I'm holy, and I alone am good because I choose to be. I can act in any way I please. I never do anything on a whim, however; I always do what's fair.

Because I'm not a human being, my thoughts aren't your thoughts, and my ways aren't your ways. Just as the heavens are higher than the earth, my thoughts are higher than your thoughts and my ways are higher than your ways.

I refuse to do anything wrong; doing what's right delights me. I'm kind to the ungrateful and the selfish. I make the sun rise on both those who do good and those who do bad. I send rain on just and unjust people alike. I'm impartial, and I can't be bribed. As surely as the sun rises every morning, I defend those who are helpless.

I say and do only what's true and wise. No one teaches and directs me. I don't need to ask anyone else for advice because I'm the source of all wisdom and knowledge.

I may seem mysterious at times, but there's a reason for everything I do. Farmers don't keep plowing their fields over and over again without planting seed, do they? Of course not. And, when the crops are ripe, farmers don't harvest all of them in the same way, do they? No—they harvest each crop in the appropriate manner, according to plan. Each of my actions is part of a bigger plan, too.

I overflow with love for those who love me. I'm faithful and merciful to them. I'm humble and gentle with them, and slow to get angry. My anger

I want to make an agreement with you (3)

toward those who work against me, however, is like a fire that burns all the time. 13

If I say I'm going to do something, I do it; my words are never empty or meaningless. When rain or snow falls, it falls for a reason—it waters the earth. My words and actions, like the rain and the snow, accomplish what I intend. No one can stand in the way of what I say or do. 14

All living things pass away, like grass or flowers in a field. Grass withers and flowers fade when a hot wind blows on them, but not even one of my words loses its power or meaning. Heaven and earth may disappear, but my words last forever. 15

I made the world good

Out of darkness, water, and emptiness, I made an orderly world. "Let there be light," I said, and there was light. I saw that the light was good, so I separated it from the darkness, making both day and night.

"Let the waters be kept in two separate places," I said, and they were. I made the sky to separate the waters above it from the waters below it.

"Let the waters below the sky be gathered together, and let dry land appear," I said, and the land was separated by the seas. I saw that it was good. "Let vegetation that's capable of reproducing itself grow on the earth," I said, and it was so. I saw that it was good.

"Let there be lights in the heavens," I said. "They'll distinguish day from night and season from season." It was so, and I saw that it was good.

"Let swarms of living things live and grow in the waters, and let birds fly in the skies," I said, and it was so. I saw that they were good. I blessed them, saying, "Be fruitful and multiply. Fill the seas and the heavens."

"Let many different kinds of creatures live and grow on the land," I said, and it was so. I saw that it was good.

Then I created human beings in my own image, and blessed them, saying, "Be fruitful and multiply. I'm putting you in charge of the fish in the sea, the birds of the air, and every living thing that moves on the earth."

I saw what I had made, and everything was very good.

Your responsibilities

Ever since I first made human beings, I've explained that it's in your best interests to keep the world good. You do this by learning to tell right from wrong, good from bad, and then doing what's right and good. Just as you hunger and thirst for food and drink, I want you to crave things that are good for you.

It's important that you try your hardest to keep from doing anything bad or wrong. You must feel so strongly about this that even the sight of another person doing something wrong is enough to make you sad.

I don't want anyone to have trouble distinguishing right from wrong or good from bad. That's why I've clearly explained the differences between them. I've even spelled out specific guidelines for you to follow. People who live by them do what's good and right; people who don't do what's bad and wrong. It's as simple as that.

I've explained that for your own good it's necessary to carefully learn and follow these guidelines. You must not turn away from them even in the slightest, or add to or subtract from them. This isn't too difficult or tiring for you; it isn't beyond your

reach or strength. I'm asking you to do something I
know you're capable of doing.

I've offered to make an agreement with you if
you're willing. I want to have a relationship with you
in which we love and trust each other. I promise to
keep my part of the agreement if you promise to keep
yours. My offer applies not only to you, but also to
your children and your children's children.

In order to keep your part of the agreement, all
you have to do is carefully follow my guidelines. You
must never forget about them or disregard them.
Then I'll keep mine—I'll give you the good life that
lasts forever. If you break your part of the agreement, however, I'll have to break mine, too.

Because I care about you, I want you to take
seriously what I'm saying. Losing the good life is no
small matter. You hurt yourself when you refuse to
live according to my guidelines. I'll explain this.

When you do wrong over and over again, even if
you don't mean to, your thinking becomes twisted.
Eventually, you can't tell right from wrong whether
you want to or not. Imagine that you touch something clean with something dirty. Does the dirty
thing become clean when it touches the clean thing?
Of course not—just the opposite happens. In the
same way, even the smallest amount of bad in you, if
it isn't stopped right away, can spread throughout
your entire being until you're completely corrupt.
You can wash the outside of your body with the
strongest soap all day long, but it won't make you
clean again.

When you contaminate yourself by continually
doing things that are bad or wrong, you separate
yourself from me. I can no longer keep my agreement with you, so I don't give you the good life
anymore. You end up bringing so many problems
down on your own head that you can't get out from
under them all by yourself.

You do it to yourself

Imagine that you're on trial for breaking a law. Pretend that I'm the judge. I give you the opportunity to plead your case using your strongest arguments. I listen to the witnesses both for and against you.

During your trial, I carefully try to find out the truth of the matter. Because I'm God, you can't hide anything from me. I know everything about you, both good and bad; I know when you sit down or stand up, when you come in or go out.

Whatever you try to hide is brought out into the open. I know all your secrets. The words you've said in the dark are now heard in the daylight. The things you've whispered in a private room are now shouted from the rooftops. You can't keep anything from me.

When I've heard all the evidence, I make a decision based on your behavior. The things you yourself have said and done determine what the verdict will be.

Of course, your relationship with me doesn't take place in a courtroom, yet I make decisions about you every moment of every day. If you're doing good, you bring good upon yourself; if you're not doing good, you bring bad upon yourself. Eventually, everything you say and do comes back to help or hurt you.

If I decide that you haven't been faithful to your part of the agreement between us, it's because you've done more than enough bad things to make me feel this way. Rather than look out for you, I sit back and let you hurt yourself. I allow problems to spring up for you like poisonous weeds in a field. They can end up destroying you as a hot desert wind dries up everything in its path.

Don't blame me when you suffer the consequences of your own bad behavior. When you disregard your part of the agreement, you bring trouble upon yourself. It's your fault, not mine!

It's your choice

In order to live the good life, then, you must choose to follow the guidelines I've set up for you. No one else can do this for you, and you can't do it for somebody else, either. A person can't keep my agreement for anyone but himself or herself. Parents can't even do it for their children. Your own behavior determines whether you live the good life or not.

Some people blame their parents for their troubles—but that's foolish! It's been said that when parents eat sour grapes, their children's teeth are set on edge. This isn't true. The children's teeth are set on edge only when they themselves eat sour grapes, not when their parents do. In the same way, if they don't live the good life, it's because they do things that are wrong, not because their parents do.

If parents who keep my agreement have children who don't, the children don't live the good life. On the other hand, if these same children grow up and have children of their own who see all the bad things their parents are doing, and choose to follow the guidelines I've set up instead of imitating their parents, they will live the good life even though their parents don't.

Unfortunately, children often learn their parents' bad habits and bring trouble upon themselves. Some people say that these children suffer because of their parents' words and deeds. This isn't true. They suffer because they themselves do what's wrong and harmful. If instead they'd choose to keep my agreement, they'd live the good life.

If you aren't living the good life, it's no one's fault but your own. Another person can't give the good life to you or take it away from you. If you choose not to live according to the guidelines I've set up for you, you suffer the consequences of your own harmful words and deeds.

You need to become a new person

You may want to follow my guidelines but find that you're unable to. If this is the case, it's because you're tied to the past. You may no longer be capable of deciding to do right instead of wrong; you may be a prisoner of your own twisted thinking.

Don't give up if this seems to be the case. Even if you can't help yourself, I can help you. I can save you from your own twisted thinking and show you how to become a new person.

Before I can do this, however, you must decide that you *want* to be a new person. Making this choice is like following a hard path to a narrow door that few people find. Most people go along an easy path to a wide door that leads nowhere. If you want to live the good life, you must disregard what other people are doing. You must choose to walk this hard path and go through this narrow door. You must choose to become a new person.

I don't mean this literally, of course—that you have to go back into your mother and come out again. I'm talking about something else entirely. When you're controlled by your own twisted thinking, you need to turn yourself around and make a fresh start. Unless you do this, you can't live the good life.

I'll explain how you can become a new person.

II
HOW TO BECOME A NEW PERSON

First, make things right with me

Before you can become a new person, you must take an honest look at yourself. Think carefully about the things you've said and done in the past. Don't make excuses for your bad behavior. Admit it. Be sorry for what you've done wrong.

By breaking my agreement, you turn your back on me. So you have to make peace with me. Look everywhere for me with all your heart and soul. When you find me, ask me to listen to you. Then admit to me the wrong things you've said and done. Your prayer could be something like this:

God, I've taken an honest look at myself, and while I see that I have many good points, I also recognize my bad ones. I admit the things I've done wrong and I'm sorry for them. Please forgive me and help me to be the kind of person you want me to be. I realize that no one but you can give me the good life. From now on, I won't let anyone or anything else be more important to me than you are. I'll do my best to follow the guidelines you've set up for me. Amen.

Next, make things right with other people

In addition to making peace with me, you must do what you can to make peace with people you've wronged. For example, if you cheated or robbed someone, if you found something another person lost and then lied about it, or if you gave false information, try to right whatever you did wrong. Give back what you got by cheating or stealing. Return what doesn't belong to you. Try to undo the trouble you caused by giving false information. If you've done anything else to harm another person, make amends for it.

It's not enough to make peace with me if you don't also try to make peace with other people. Doing something wrong to another person is the same as doing something wrong to me. You must straighten things out with both me and other people before I'll forgive you and give you the good life.

I forgive you

Once you've made things right with both me and other people, I'll forgive you for the bad things you've done in the past. This story will help you to understand what I mean.

A man had two sons. The younger son came to him and said, "Father, you told me that someday you'd give me part of your property. I'd like to have it now." So the man divided his property and gave the younger son his share.

After a few days, the younger son sold what his father had given him and left home with the money. He traveled to a far country, where he wasted his money on loose living. Soon the younger son had spent every cent he had and couldn't buy food for himself. He had to take a job feeding pigs. He was so hungry that even the pigs' food looked good to him, but no one would give him anything to eat.

The younger son finally came to his senses and said to himself, "The people who work for my father have more than enough to eat, and here I am starving to death. I'll go back to my father and say to him, 'Father, I've behaved badly. I no longer deserve to be called your son. Please take me back, but treat me like one of your employees.'"

The younger son started home. While he was still a long way down the road, his father saw him coming and his heart went out to him. The father ran to his younger son and hugged and kissed him.

"Father," the son said, "I'm sorry for what I've done. I no longer deserve to be called your son."

But the father said to his employees, "Hurry and find the best clothes in the house for my son. Give him a ring for his finger and shoes for his feet. Then go and get my best calf and kill it. We're going to celebrate. I thought my son was dead, but he's alive. He was lost, but now he's found." So the party began.

Meanwhile, the older son, who'd been out in the field, came near the house and heard music and dancing. "What's going on?" he asked.

"Your brother's come home," an employee answered. "Your father killed his best calf and is throwing a party for him."

The older brother was furious and refused to go into the house. His father came out and begged him to come inside, but he angrily said, "All these years I've worked like a slave for you. I never once disobeyed you. Yet you didn't give me so much as a young goat so that I could have a party with my friends. Now this son of yours comes back after spending your money foolishly, and you kill your best calf for him!"

"Son," the father replied, "you've been with me

all this time and everything I have is yours. I thought your brother was dead, and he's alive. He was lost, but now he's found. How can I help but celebrate?"

The younger son left his father and squandered the money his father had given him. You, too, waste the good things I give you when you don't keep my agreement. But if you come to your senses and return to me with all your heart and soul, admitting the things you've done wrong, I welcome you back. Like the father who ran out to meet his son, I come to you as surely as the sun rises at dawn and the rain falls in the springtime.

I forgive the things you admit you've done wrong. I blot them out of my mind and never even think about them again. They disappear like morning mist at noon.

Even though the wrong things you've done in the past may have stained you, you become clean when I forgive you. It's as if I take your dirty clothes off you, wash you, and dress you in brand new clothes as beautiful as those worn by a bride and bridegroom on their wedding day.

I rejoice when you come back to me. I'm as delighted as a person who's lost something precious and then found it again.

If a woman who has ten silver coins loses one of them, she turns on the light and cleans her whole house, looking everywhere until she finds it. Then she calls in her friends and neighbors, saying, "Be happy with me, for I've found the coin I thought I'd lost."

When a man who owns a hundred sheep loses one of them, he leaves the other ninety-nine sheep and searches for the lost one until he finds it. Then he picks it up and happily carries it home. He calls his friends and neighbors together, saying, "Rejoice with me, for I've found my lost sheep."

Just as the woman celebrates when she finds her coin, and the man when he finds his sheep, I rejoice

How to become a new person

when you come back to me. I'm happier when you make things right with me than I am when ninety-nine other people don't need to. 10

You're a new person

Making things right with me and with others is something you need to do every day of your life—it isn't enough to do it once or twice, or whenever you feel like getting around to it. As long as you keep admitting the things you do wrong and try your hardest to make amends for them, I keep forgiving you. It's a continuing process. 11

The more you straighten out your life, the more healthy your thinking becomes. The things in your past that prevented you from following my guidelines influence you less and less. It's as if a burden drops off your shoulders. Instead of feeling as if you're walking bent over all the time, you're able to stand up straight. You no longer do wrong whether you want to or not, which is what happens when your thinking is twisted. You're free to live according to my guidelines. 12

So do it! Be careful not to let your thinking get twisted again. Don't do what you *think* is right, or what someone else tells you is right. Keep my agreement instead. When you make a mistake, quickly admit it and try to correct it—and do your best never to make the same mistake again. 13

By following my guidelines, you bring good upon yourself. Like a potter shaping clay, I mold you into a new person. I turn misfortunes into blessings. I make plans for your well-being, and give you hope for the future. I enjoy being good to you. 14

Rather than being at odds with each other, you and I love and trust each other. I treat you as if you'd never done anything wrong, and I keep my part of the agreement by giving you the good life. 15

What happens if you turn away from me again?

As long as you keep living by my guidelines, I'm pleased with you. You're as delightful to me as grapes found unexpectedly in the wilderness, or the first fruits of a fig tree. If, on the other hand, you turn away from me again, I'm disappointed in you. You're no longer the kind of person I want you to be. You're like silver that's full of impurities, or wine mixed with water.

If someone told you that the snow had disappeared from the tops of the tallest mountains, would you believe it? Or if you heard that all the streams in the world had dried up, would you think that was true? Of course not! In the same way, I find it hard to believe that you would ever turn away from me again—especially after experiencing the good life.

This sort of thing reminds me of the son who turned against his own father. The father was devoted to him—he held his infant son in his arms, helped him learn how to walk, bent down to feed him, and carefully taught him right from wrong. The father dreamed about how he would one day give his son everything he owned. He was sure that his son would grow up to be proud of his father and would never turn away from him. Instead, the son rejected his own father and even plotted against him! The father couldn't believe it.

I care for you even when you cause problems for yourself. I'm there to help you and advise you whenever you need me. I bless you and give you the good life. You prosper because of me. That's why I'm amazed that you would even think of turning away from me. You only end up hurting yourself.

Imagine that a vine deliberately turns away from the light. Does it keep growing? Of course not! Its roots die and its leaves wither; eventually, it's so weak that the slightest breeze blows it away. If you reject everything that's good for you, you're like that vine; you die as surely as it does.

How to become a new person

When you carefully live according to my guidelines, you become both happy and wise. It's as if you live in my garden with me. We talk to each other, and I look out for you; you wear beautiful clothes that I've given you and never lack anything.

As you live the good life and prosper, be careful not to lose sight of the fact that this is happening because you've chosen to keep my agreement. Never become lax or let yourself be convinced that you can stop living by my guidelines. If you get rich and become proud, or if you get powerful and use your power for your own ends, you break my agreement and go right back to where you started from before you agreed to follow me. I take away the blessings I've given you, and you no longer live the good life. **23**

You may think that I'm unfair if I do this to someone who used to follow me. Who's really unfair—I, or the person who turns away from me? I'm not the one who breaks the agreement in the first place.

If people who used to do wrong do their best to make amends and carefully keep my agreement, I reward them with the good life. If, on the other hand, people who used to live according to my guidelines decide that they no longer will, they can't expect the good things they received in the past. **24**

Those who turn away from me after having kept my agreement can actually end up in worse shape than if they'd never followed me at all. I'll give you an example of what I'm saying to help you understand.

A man had a bad habit. He got rid of the bad habit, but didn't replace it with a good one. Slowly but surely, he fell back into his old ways, and even picked up a few more bad habits in the process. Eventually, he was in worse shape than he was when he had only one bad habit.

If people aren't careful to keep following my guidelines, they soon go back to their old ways. They may end up doing more harm to themselves than they would have if they'd never even heard about me and my agreement. This can happen to you.

What my guidelines are

I've been talking about the guidelines I've set up for you to follow so that you'll live the good life. But what exactly *are* these guidelines?

They're so simple that they can all be put into one sentence: Love me with all your heart, soul, strength, and mind, and love others as you love yourself.

It may be hard from time to time for you to know how to do this in specific situations. Because I want it to be as easy as possible for you to keep my agreement, I'll spell out my guidelines in detail for you. First, I'll discuss how to love me. Then I'll talk about how to love others.

III
HOW TO LOVE ME

Remember that I'm the only true God

I'm the only true God. There's no other God but me. I won't share this position, and I won't tolerate your thinking that anyone or anything else is more important to you than I am. You must not worship false gods.

Some people think that the term "false gods" only refers to images made of stone, metal, or wood, but this isn't true. Of course, a false god can be an image that people fall down in front of and worship, but it can also be money, social position, another person, or even yourself. Basically, a false god is anything that takes my place in your life and prevents you from keeping my agreement.

It's impossible for you to serve both me and a false god at the same time. Either you'll love me and neglect it, or you'll neglect me and love it. You have to choose between us. If it looks as if you're about to make something into a false god, get rid of it or change your thinking.

4 False gods aren't in any way like me. They can't explain the past or predict the future; they can't do bad or good; they can't give you advice. I'd be willing to let them argue their case, but they can't hear or speak. They're worthless. They're nothing more than delusions in the minds of those who worship them. They're as empty as the wind. The person who chooses them over me, even in secret, is a fool.

Don't ever be foolish enough to worship images or symbols. Don't plant trees and bow down before them, or erect pillars or carved stones and pray to them as if they were gods. Don't even make something that's supposed to represent me and plan to worship it. You don't know what I look like!

Images are things that people make, and nothing more. Think about how wooden idols are made, for example. People cut down trees and use part of the wood to heat their homes and cook their food. They they use another part of it to make a god! Carpenters mark the wood with pencils and compasses and shape it with tools. They fasten it with nails so it won't fall over. Then people bow down and **5** worship it! Can you see how ridiculous this is?

Some people are so poor that they can't afford to buy or make wooden idols for themselves, so they worship trees instead. They carve images on them, and then convince themselves that the trees are their gods. How can anyone possibly think that a tree has power to solve problems simply because something's carved on it?

Worshiping metal is as absurd as worshiping wood. People take gold or silver out of their own pockets and then give it to workers they hire. The workers are supposed to turn the gold or silver into gods. The workers are only human; they get hungry and thirsty just like other people do. How can the gods that they make be compared to me?

The people who hired the workers to make the idols come and get them. Then they carry the idols home with them and fall down and worship them.

How to love me

The gods just stand there because they can't move. They're like scarecrows in a field; they can't speak, walk, or breathe. They have to be carried wherever they go. How terrible for the people who ask them for help! Idols can't even hear, much less get rid of people's troubles for them.   6

Some people believe in evil spirits and even worship them. Don't let these people influence you in any way, and don't be talked into worshiping evil spirits yourself.   7

I made the sun, moon, and stars, but they aren't gods, either. Be careful not to worship them. Don't worry about what seem to be signs in the heavens, even if other people do.   8

People around you may have many different kinds of false gods, and may even seem to have good reasons for serving them. Regardless of what these people say or do, however, don't let them sway you. Be careful not to be misled into turning away from me to follow a lie, even for a second. Always remember that I'm the only true God, and that you should worship only me.

It isn't *where* but *how* you worship me that matters. I want you to worship me with your attitude and thoughts as well as your actions.   9

Ornaments and show don't impress or please me; neither do rituals like prostitution for religious reasons. If you make an altar for me, keep it simple. Be sure that a building dedicated to me is used as a house of prayer for all people. Don't set up idols in it or let politics influence how it's used. Don't let people misuse it for purposes other than serving me, or turn it into a place for traders or robbers.   10

11, 12

Love me completely

The best way to worship me, of course, is to love me. I want you to love me with all your heart, soul, strength, and mind. This means depending on me

and trusting me completely. Come to me for comfort
and advice. Feel free to test me to find out whether
13. or not I keep my promises.

I'll give you some examples of what I mean. A
merchant was searching for fine pearls. When he
found one pearl of great value, he went and sold all
that he had so he could buy that single pearl. In the
same way, a woman who found a treasure in a field
sold everything she owned so she could buy the field.
14 I want you to be just as committed to me.

Think of me as a vine, and of yourself as one of
the branches. A branch can't bear fruit if it's cut off
from the vine, and neither can you live the good life
if you're cut off from me. So do whatever you can to
keep our loving and trusting relationship alive and
15 help it to grow.

Be one with me so that I'm in you and you're in
me. When you eat bread or drink wine, it becomes
part of you. When you live according to the guidelines I've set up for you, I become part of you, too.
16 This is the kind of relationship I'd like us to have.

Be my servant

17,   I made you a human being, but I still want you
18, to be as much like me as you can. So try your best to
19, act as I'd act and do my work in the world. Tell the
20, truth about me. Set an example for other people to
21 follow. Show them what it's like to keep my agreement and live the good life.

Start living according to my guidelines right
now. Don't ever try to hide the fact that you're
following me. Be like a city that can be seen from all
directions because it's built on top of a hill, or like a
bright light that can't be covered or turned off. A
person doesn't hide a lamp under a bed, but sets it on
a table so it can light the whole room. Let the light
that's in you because of me shine, too, so that people
22 can get to know me through you.

How to love me (21)

If you turn away from me and refuse to live according to my guidelines, you're like salt that loses its saltiness. You don't do yourself or anyone else any good. So carefully listen to me, learn from me, and do your best to understand me. The more you think about and study my words, the more you benefit from them. 23, 24, 25, 26

Serve me with all your heart and soul, doing everything I tell you to do. Make it clear to those who refuse to follow me just how much you love me. If you try to be as much like me as you can, anyone who knows you will also know me. Someone who thinks highly of you will also think highly of me. 27, 28

Being my servant is a joyful task, so sing and rejoice in everything you do. Think of keeping my agreement as a privilege rather than a hardship. Even though you may give up certain things in order to follow my guidelines, you'll gain much more in return—the good life. 29

Fight what's wrong

I want you to do your best to get rid of what's bad in yourself and the world. If you try to do this on your own, however, you'll end up fighting a losing battle; you need my help. 30

Don't cover up things that you know are wrong or harmful or make excuses for them. They won't go away just because you ignore them. Recognize them for what they are. 31

Fight against the love of false gods, hypocrisy, pride, and unkindness. Do your best to overcome oppression, injustice, lies, violence, and other bad things. Work together with other people who keep my agreement to make the world a better place. 32, 33

You may feel that it's impossible to get rid of all the bad things in yourself and the world, but don't give up! Never let yourself get sidetracked. Above all, don't be afraid to stand up for what you know is right. Keep in mind that I'm always with you, and I'll give you the strength you need.

Don't ever be afraid of what other people say or do. They may threaten you and even hurt your body, but they can't harm you in any other way. There's only one thing in the whole world that you ever need be afraid of—the possibility that you might break my agreement and cut yourself off from me.

Sparrows are sold for pennies in the marketplace, but not one of them falls to the ground without my knowing about it. You're much more valuable to me than sparrows are—I even know how many hairs you have on your head. So how can you worry that I won't take care of you? If you live according to the guidelines I've set up for you, you've nothing to fear.

Instead of being weak and afraid, become strong and brave. Keep my agreement no matter what's happening around you. Do whatever needs to be done to conquer the bad things in yourself and the world, and gain the good life I've promised you.

Always look at the present as preparation for the future. If you can't even walk, you'll certainly never be able to run. If you fall down when you're on open ground, how can you ever hope to find your way through a jungle? So do your best to grow stronger every day in service to me.

Don't be naïve in your battle against what's bad, or let your guard down even for a second. Don't get cynical, though; try to be as trusting and loving as you can under the circumstances. Be careful not to waste the resources I've given you, or tell something that's important to you to a person who could use it against you. That would be like throwing pearls to pigs.

Pray to me

I encourage you to pray to me and ask for whatever you want or need. Before you pray, however, make things right with the people around you. Tell anyone who's wronged you that you forgive him or her, and ask anyone you've wronged to forgive you.

Don't be like hypocrites who love to stand up and pray in churches and synagogues or on street corners where other people can see and hear them. This attention from others is all the reward they'll ever get. When you pray, go into a room by yourself, shut the door, and talk to me in secret.

When you want something from me, don't just say, "Please, God, give this to me," or "Please, God, make this happen." Ask for what you think I'd want you to have, keeping my guidelines in mind while you're praying. Remember to say, "God, may your will be done."

Believe, without doubting, that I'll answer you when you pray according to my will. The more closely you follow my guidelines, the more likely you'll be to pray for what I'd want you to have and get it.

Pray for the people who keep my agreement, and pray for the people who don't. Keep reminding me of my promise to give you the good life and make the world a better place.

Some people believe that I listen to them whenever they pray regardless of how they pray. They themselves don't pay attention to what they're saying, but they expect me to. They use a lot of words, or they recite the same words over and over again without giving any thought at all to what these words mean. Be careful not to pray as they do! Instead, think of what you're saying when you talk to me. You may want to pray something like this:

God, may everyone give you the respect you deserve, worship only you, and follow you. Give all of us what we need for today. Forgive us for what we've done wrong, just as we forgive other people who've wronged us. Don't test us too hard, but free us from the things that could harm us or keep us from living according to your guidelines. Amen.

Keep the Sabbath

Take one day each week as a day of rest and dedicate it to me. Do your work during the other six days. In this way, you, your children, your employees, and everyone else associated with you will have an opportunity to rest and become refreshed every week.

I've given you the Sabbath for your benefit, and you can decide how best to use it. Don't get involved with ridiculous laws that dictate what you can and can't do. Use common sense. If there's something you know you should do, go ahead and do it. For example, if an animal falls into a pit, pull it out. If your cattle need water, give it to them. If people come to you for help, help them. Don't use the Sabbath as an excuse to avoid responsibilities.

In general, though, don't carry on business as usual or do anything unnecessary. For example, prepare your food on the day before the Sabbath so you don't have to cook and bake on that day. Spend the Sabbath delightfully.

Using one day a week in this way will be a sign of the agreement between you and me. It'll give you time to rest and think about the special relationship you have with me.

Don't be a hypocrite

I've been telling you about myself and the agreement I'm willing to make with you. Don't misuse this knowledge. By this I mean that you mustn't do something wrong and claim that it's all right because you're doing it in my name, or say that something bad is actually good when you know better. People who do this sort of thing are hypocrites, and they're guilty of taking my name in vain.

If you say that you follow me when you really don't, you're a hypocrite, and I won't give you the good life. People around you will wonder why things aren't going well for you, and they may even blame me for your problems. This gives me a bad reputation.

Hypocrites make me angry because they say one thing and do another. They claim to praise me, but they're really only praising themselves. They take advantage of other people while pretending to help them. They lie and cheat, and then cover up their actions with long prayers.

Hypocrites may seem to be good, but don't let them fool you. They're like beautiful tombs full of nothing but bones. They're like people who only wash the outside of a cup for the sake of appearances and never wash the inside.

Some hypocrites say that they can accurately interpret my words, but they can't because they don't really know anything about me. Instead, they take what they think they know and use it for their own purposes. This, too, gives me a bad reputation.

Some hypocrites claim to honor people who were persecuted for openly following me. They even go so far as to build monuments to those who were martyred, and say, "If only we'd been alive then! We never would have let that happen. We would have tried to save those people." What nonsense! If I sent my servants to them right now, they wouldn't even recognize them. Instead, they'd ridicule them, chase them from town to town, and even kill them.

Even some religious leaders are hypocrites. They love to wear clerical clothes and be treated as if they're better than other people. They like to have special titles attached to their names, and they want people to call them by these titles. They do anything they can to be noticed by others.

Hypocritical religious leaders don't teach people

to distinguish right from wrong and help them to do what's right. Instead, they take away from or add to my guidelines to suit their own purposes. They crush people with difficult demands that have nothing to do with following me and that they themselves don't meet. These kinds of religious leaders keep the truth about me from people; they don't live the good life, and they keep others from living it, too. They travel all over the world to make converts who become 57 even worse than they themselves are.

Only a hypocritical religious leader would say, "It's all right to break a promise if you must. But if you make a promise in God's name, you have to keep it." How ridiculous this is! A promise is a promise whether it's made in my name or not. You 58 shouldn't have to strengthen your words with a vow.

Some hypocrites brag about how much money they give me, but they don't bother to show their love for me in any other way. They think that their money can make up for the bad things they say and do. Can someone buy my forgiveness? Of course not. Naturally, I want people to use their money to do my work in the world, but that's only a small part of loving me. Giving money to me while ignoring me in every other way is like straining out a gnat only to 59 swallow a camel.

How can you keep from becoming a hypocrite? Watch out for people like the ones I've just described, and don't let them influence you in any way. Even a little hypocrisy can affect your thinking 60 as yeast does dough.

Respect me so much that you do everything I tell you to do. Don't complain about me or speak out against me. Be careful never to hurt my reputation 61, in the world.
62 Don't keep my agreement just so other people will compliment you for it. For example, if you fast—that is, if you stop eating for a while for spiritual reasons—don't be like the hypocrites who look

sad and bedraggled so that other people will notice they're fasting. Recognition from others is the only reward they'll ever receive. When you fast, wash your face and comb your hair so that no one will know you're hungry. Let it be a secret between you and me. 63

If you make a promise, keep it. Don't swear by me, by heaven, by earth, or by a city; swearing by something or someone can't make your promise more meaningful. What good does it do to base your promise on something you have no control over, and that has no relationship to the promise itself? When you promise something, just say a simple yes or no to seal the agreement. That's enough. 64

Be humble

Don't walk around with a haughty attitude. Instead, be humble. Behave as if the least important person you know is really the most important. This story will help you to understand what I mean. 65

Two men went to the temple to pray. One was a religious leader and the other was a tax collector. The religious leader said, "God, I thank you that I'm not like that tax collector over there. I fast twice a week, and I give ten percent of everything I earn to you."

The tax collector stood off in a corner not daring to look up. He pounded his chest, saying, "God, have mercy on me. I've done wrong and I'm sorry." Which person do *you* think I listened to? The religious leader or the tax collector? Which one was humble and asked my forgiveness? The tax collector, of course. The religious leader was much too proud to admit that he'd done anything wrong. 66

If you happen to have a special title or an important position, don't think that you're better than everyone else just because of this. All of you are

equal in my eyes. Don't allow or encourage other people to look to you instead of me for guidance;
67 each of you should follow only me.

Don't try to attract attention to yourself, or it may backfire. For example, some people will go to a reception and sit in the best seats so that others will notice them. Be careful not to do that sort of thing yourself, or you may regret it. If someone more important than you arrives, the host or hostess may come over to you and ask you to give up your seat to the newcomer, and you'll be embarrassed. So sit in a less conspicuous place to begin with, and you'll feel much better about things. Who knows—the host or hostess may even come over to you and insist that
68 you take one of the best seats.

Don't think for a minute that I give you the good life because you're better than other people— you aren't. I give you the good life because I keep my part of the agreement when you keep yours. I don't give the good life to people who refuse to live accord-
69 ing to my guidelines.

Remember all your days that without me your thinking would be so twisted that you couldn't live
70 the good life even if you wanted to. So don't become proud of yourself when I give you wisdom, riches, and strength. Be happy, instead, that things are right
71 between you and me.

Don't brag about the fact that you keep my agreement. If your employees do what you pay them to do, should you have to praise them constantly? Of course not. You shouldn't expect compliments for following me, either. After all, you're only doing
72 what's in your own best interests.

Don't try to buy the good life

Don't waste your time or energy acquiring material things; they can be destroyed, lost, or sto-

How to love me

len. Instead, concentrate on gathering spiritual treasures that last forever. 73

For example, there was once a rich man who thought that money was everything. One year his land produced so many crops that his barns couldn't hold them all after the harvest. "I'll tear down my barns and build even bigger ones," he said proudly. "I'll be so wealthy that I'll never have to worry about anything again! I'll finally be able to sit back and enjoy myself." How foolish the rich man was! He thought that money could guarantee his happiness. He died that night, and nothing he owned was worth anything to him after that. 74

How hard it is for rich people to live according to my guidelines! It's easier for a camel to go through the eye of a needle than it is for rich people to trust me instead of money to give them the good life. 75

So that you won't be tempted to rely only on material things, I encourage you to share what you have with other people. Spend your time and energy working for spiritual treasures that don't wear out and can't be stolen or destroyed. The treasures you accumulate show what kind of person you are. 76

The good life involves much more than material things. Look at the birds in the air, for example; they don't plant or harvest, yet I feed them. Don't you think that you're worth more to me than they are? Look at the lilies in the field; the richest people in the world aren't dressed as well as they are. If I clothe even the flowers, which grow in the fields one day and fade the next, how can you possibly think that I won't take care of you? You can't add a single moment to your life by worrying, so why worry? I know that you need material things like food, drink, and clothes. If you live according to my guidelines, you'll get them, along with everything else you need, too. 77

Don't worry about tomorrow. Let tomorrow take care of itself. Live one day at a time. 78

This doesn't mean, however, that you can be irresponsible. On the contrary, I want you to use the things you have wisely and carefully. Keep in mind, though, that everything you have really belongs to me. The whole universe is mine because I made it. I expect you to take good care of the things I've given to you.

This story will help you to understand what I mean.

A rich man decided that a man he'd hired to handle his affairs was mismanaging them. He called the man to him. "I no longer want you to be my steward," he said. "Turn in an account of how you've managed my finances and then leave."

"What did I do wrong?" the steward wanted to know.

"You didn't try hard enough to collect debts that other people owe me," the rich man said. "Now it's been so long that I'll probably never get anything at all out of those people."

"What can I do about this?" the steward asked himself. "I want to keep my job." He thought for a while, and then said, "I'll try something. It can't hurt, and it might help."

The steward called in each person who was in debt to his employer. "How much do you owe?" he asked the first one.

"Nine hundred gallons of oil," the man said.

"Take your contract and sit down," said the steward. "I'll let you cross out nine hundred gallons and write in four hundred and fifty instead if you pay me for the four hundred and fifty gallons right now. Then we'll consider the debt paid in full." The man did what the steward told him to do.

"How much do you owe?" the steward asked another man.

"Nine hundred bushels of wheat," the man said.

"Here's your contract," the steward said. "You

can cross out nine hundred bushels and write in seven hundred instead if you pay me today for the seven hundred. Then we'll consider the matter settled." This man did what the steward told him to do, too.

The steward talked in turn to all the people who'd been in debt to his employer for a long time and didn't seem likely ever to pay him. Then he went back to the rich man and said, "Even though you fired me, I thought I'd see what I could do about the unpaid loans you've made to people. Here's what I managed to collect—at least half of what these people owed you. It isn't everything, but it's better than nothing."

The rich man admired the steward for being so clever, and let him keep his job. The steward showed more wisdom in handling his affairs than many people who follow me do. I want you to be wise like him and carefully take care of the things you have.

The more I give you, the more I expect of you. Even if something I give you seems insignificant, I want you to take good care of it. If you don't wisely use what you have, you'll lose it.

For example, there was once a man who planned to take a trip to a distant country. Before leaving, he distributed money to three of his employees and told them to manage it while he was gone. He gave $5,000 to one, $2,000 to another, and $1,000 to still another.

The employee who'd been given $5,000 invested it and made $5,000 more. The employee who'd been given $2,000 invested it and made $2,000 more. But the employee who'd been given $1,000 took the money and buried it in a hole in the ground.

When the man returned, he wanted to know how his employees had managed his money. The first and second employees came to him and explained how they'd doubled their original investments. The man congratulated them both. "Well done!" he said. "Now I'll put you in charge of even larger sums of money."

The third employee came forward and said, "Sir, I took your thousand dollars and buried it in a hole in the ground. That way, I didn't risk losing it, and I always knew where it was."

"I can't believe it!" the man exclaimed. "Why didn't you at least invest it in a bank so it could draw interest?" He motioned to another employee. "Take the thousand dollars and give it to the person who made the most money for me while I was gone."

"But, sir," the employee said, "that person already has ten thousand dollars."

"You're right," the man said. "Those who sensibly use what they have get even more, but those who don't lose even the little they think they have."

If, like the first two employees, you wisely use what I've given you, I'll see that you get even more. If, on the other hand, you act like the third employee and don't take good care of the things I've given you, I'll take them and everything else you think you have away from you.

Give me tithes and offerings

I want you to return one-tenth of your income to me. Remember that what you have is mine to begin with, and that I'm only letting you use it. In addition to your tithe, give me generous offerings according to how much I bless you.

Several rich people once walked by a collection box in a church. Each put a large amount of money into the box. Then a poor widow came along and dropped in two coins—all she had. This poor widow gave more to me than all the rich people put together. They gave what they could easily spare,

How to love me (33)

but she put in everything she had. I want you to give to me as generously as she did. 85

Take your tithes and offerings out of the first fruits of what you produce—I don't want leftovers. 86 Don't hold back what really belongs to me or give me things that are flawed. I don't want you to resent the 87 fact that you should give me tithes and offerings. Instead, thank me because you have something to give me. Be happy and praise me. Your prayer could be like this:

> God, I turned to you when I was unhappy. You forgave me for the things I'd done wrong, and gave me the good life. Thank you very much. Here are my tithes and offerings, which really belong to you. Amen. 88

After giving your tithes and offerings to me, see that they're used to help strangers, orphans, those who are alone, and other people in need. Giving to them is the same as giving to me. If you're generous with others, you'll receive even more than you give. Imagine a basket full of leaves that have been pressed down and shaken together and still overflow the sides of the basket. That's how much you'll get in return for being kind to others. 89

When you help others, don't blow your own horn like hypocrites who want to be complimented. Praise is the only reward they'll ever get. When you give to people, do it so secretly that your left hand doesn't know what your right hand is doing. I know all your secrets, and I'll reward you. 90

After you've helped others, pray something like this:

> God, I've given you my tithes and offerings, and seen to it that they've been used for people in need. I've done all that you asked me to do. Please keep blessing me with the good life. Amen. 91

Take good care of the earth and its creatures

I've given you authority over all animals, birds, creeping things, and fish. Use this power wisely. Show a reverent, compassionate concern for everything I've made so you don't pollute or otherwise harm the world. Take from the earth only what you need; don't be wasteful or irresponsible.

For example, if you're going to kill animals for food, don't kill both a mother and her young at the same time. If you're going to kill the young, let the mother go; if you're going to kill the mother, first make sure that the young are old enough to survive on their own. Don't kill the young in front of their mother or the mother in front of her young.

If you have a disagreement with someone, keep the environment out of it. For example, don't destroy trees or farmlands just to get even with someone. Are the trees or farms your enemies? Of course not. Even when you're in the midst of a difference of opinion, remember that the earth belongs to me and I want you to take good care of it.

If an animal is injured or lost, do what you can to help it regardless of how you feel about its owner. For example, if you see that someone's cow has fallen down, get help for it even if its owner doesn't like you. If you notice someone's horse wandering away, don't pretend that you can't see what's happening. Take it back to its owner. If its owner lives far from you or if you don't know who the owner is, care for the animal yourself until you can find its owner. Then give it back.

I also want you to be careful with the land. Plant and reap your crops and gather fruit from your vineyards for six years, and then let the land rest during the seventh year. If food grows on this land by itself during the seventh year, however, it's all right if you eat it.

Take good care of yourself

Keep your body, your clothes, and the things you eat and drink clean. Stay away from anything that's unhealthy or contaminated. Carefully wash after any contact with a bodily excretion and wash whatever the excretion touches. Separate toilet areas from living areas.

Don't touch a dead body unless you have to. If you do, wash yourself carefully afterward. When a dead body has been removed from a room, wash the whole room, including all the furnishings and any containers in it that don't have fastened covers.

If you get sick, go to people trained in medicine so that your illness can be treated at an early stage. Carefully follow their advice. If your illness is contagious, warn others that you're sick and stay away from them. When you're well again, wash your clothes and bathe yourself before associating with other people.

Stay away from people who have contagious diseases. Do your part to develop a system that encourages sick people to warn healthy people about their illnesses. See that sick people are isolated from others until they're well again.

Keep your living quarters clean. Get rid of mold or rot in buildings and mildew in garments you own or use. Call in an expert to help if necessary.

I've given you many things to eat. Learn to tell the difference between those that are good for you and those that aren't. Then eat only the things that are good for you. For example, don't eat contaminated meat or anything you're unsure of—throw it away instead. Don't eat an animal that's died by itself, has been killed by other animals, or for any reason hasn't been properly slaughtered. Use common sense in choosing the foods you'll eat.

Taking care of yourself is an important part of

109, loving me, as are all the other guidelines I've just
110, described for you. It's not enough to love me, how-
111 ever; before I can give you the good life, you must
also love other people as you love yourself. Remember that loving others is the same as loving me. I'll spell out the guidelines that explain how to love other people so you'll understand what I mean.

IV
HOW TO LOVE OTHER PEOPLE

Love others as you love yourself

When you love other people, you're kind to them and they can depend on you. You work hard to make peace with them. You help them when they need help, even if they don't come to you for it. You love them as you love yourself, and as I love you.

This story will help you to understand what I mean when I ask you to love other people.

A man who was traveling on a lonely road was attacked by robbers who stripped him, beat him, and left him half dead at the side of the road. A clergyman came along, saw the man, and passed by him on the other side of the road. A clergyman's assistant also came by, looked at the man, and kept on walking.

Eventually, a foreigner came along, saw the injured man, and felt sorry for him. He went over to the man, bandaged his wounds, and then gave him a ride to an inn where he spent the whole night caring for him.

The next morning, the foreigner gave money to the innkeeper and said, "Take good care of this man. If you spend more money than I've given you, I'll repay you."

Who do you think showed the most love to the injured man—the clergyman, the clergyman's assistant, or the foreigner? The foreigner, of course. If you love others, you'll help them whenever they're in need, just as the foreigner cared for the injured man.

You've probably heard it said that you should love your friends and hate your enemies. But how much effort does it take to love only those who love you, or do good only for those who do good for you, or speak only to those who speak to you? Even people who don't keep my agreement do that much. It's far more difficult to love people who don't love you. That's what I'm asking you to do.

I make the sun shine on both people who follow me and people who don't. I send rain for the just and the unjust alike. You must develop this same loving attitude toward others. After all, I created each of you. You're all equal in my eyes.

I want you to love your friends *and* your enemies. Be good to people who hate you. Be kind to those who say bad things about you. Pray for those who hurt you. Treat others as you'd like to be treated, not as they treat you.

Be one with others who live according to my guidelines, just as you and I are one. Don't work against each other. If you love each other, the world will see that all of you are following me.

Be forgiving

Don't judge others, and you won't be judged, either. How can you possibly see the speck in someone else's eye if you've got a log in your own eye? How can you say to someone else, "Let me take the speck out of your eye," when you can hardly see around the log in your own? First, take the log out of your own eye, and then you'll be able to see clearly enough to take the speck out of someone else's eye.

You aren't perfect, so what makes you think that you can point your finger at someone else? There's no one in the whole world who hasn't done something wrong, so not even one person has the right to throw stones at another.

If people wrong you, don't take out your anger on them or insult them. Don't hate them or try to get even with them. If someone hits you on the right cheek, turn your left cheek, too. If someone forces you to go one mile, go two miles. Be as forgiving as you can. If you're angry or mean in return, you only hurt yourself.

Instead of criticizing other people and getting angry at them when they wrong you, go to them one at a time by yourself and try to reason with each of them. If they apologize, forgive them. In this way, you'll make friends. Even if they do bad things to you seven times in a single day and turn to you each time and say, "I'm sorry," forgive them. Forgive someone as many times as he or she asks you to.

If you forgive others who wrong you, I'll forgive you for the wrong things you do, too. If you don't forgive others, I won't forgive you, either.

This story will help you to understand what I mean when I ask you to be forgiving.

A king who wanted to bring his accounts up to date discovered that one of his servants owed him a large amount of money. The man couldn't repay his debt, so the king decided that he should be punished.

The servant fell to his knees before the king, begging, "Sir, please have patience with me and I'll pay you everything I owe as soon as I can." The king felt so sorry for the servant that he released him and canceled his debt.

As soon as the servant had finished talking with

the king, he went looking for a fellow servant who owed him a small amount of money. He grabbed the man by the collar and demanded, "Pay me what you owe me!"

The fellow servant fell on the ground and cried, "Be patient with me, and I'll pay you!" But the servant refused, and had the man punished.

When the king's other servants heard about what had happened, they were horrified, and they told the king about it. The king sent for the servant and said to him, "Didn't I cancel your debt when you begged me to? You should have shown the same kindness to your fellow servant that I showed to you!"

You can imagine how angry the king was at the servant. I, too, will be angry and won't forgive you if you refuse to forgive others.

If people who've wronged you won't listen to you when you try to talk with them, go back to them and try again. This time, bring along two or three others to serve as witnesses. If the people who've wronged you still won't apologize and agree to straighten things out with you, you may need to go before a judge to clear up the problem. No matter how they respond to you, though, keep on being as kind to them as you can.

If you wrong other people, settle your differences as quickly as possible and try to make friends with them. Even if someone accuses you of doing something you didn't do, try to solve the problem before it gets out of hand. It's foolish to go to court and spend your last cent defending yourself, if you don't have to.

Lend to people in need

Don't refuse to help poor people. Freely lend them as much as they need, without looking down

How to love other people

on them. Don't charge them interest or expect anything in return for a loan. Even a person who refuses to keep my agreement will lend to someone who can repay a loan with interest. I want you to help people in need whether or not you think they can repay you. 9

If necessary, let a poor person live as a guest in your home without demanding payment for money, food, or anything else you lend to him or her. You may make a profit from anyone else who stays with you or borrows from you, but not from a poor person.

Even if a poor person can repay you for what he or she has borrowed, cancel the loan after a reasonable period of time. Don't keep him or her in debt to you forever. If you do cancel a loan, don't let that stop you from lending to that person again or to another person in need. 10

Just because someone borrows from you doesn't mean that you can treat him or her with less consideration than you would anyone else. For example, don't go into a person's house to get security for a loan unless you're invited. Stand outside and let the person to whom you're making the loan bring the collateral out to you. Be sure to return the security to the owner when the loan is repaid. Don't take as security for a loan a person's only clothes, or equipment he or she needs to make a living. Be kind and thoughtful at all times and impose as little hardship on the borrower as possible. 11

Help those less fortunate than you

Be careful not to take advantage of anyone. Don't mistreat the handicapped, and be kind to those less fortunate than you. 12

Do your best to correct the injustices you see around you. Feed the hungry, give drink to the thirsty, and give clothes to people who need them. Visit the sick and see that they're taken care of. Help those who are weak to become strong. Provide homes for the homeless poor, and visit people in prison. Comfort those who are unhappy, and encourage them rather than criticize them. Even when you do this for someone who seems unimportant, you do it for me.

Be kind to strangers, for you, too, have been a stranger and you know what it's like. Treat strangers as well as you would anyone else. For example, when you give a dinner party, don't just invite friends, relatives, or rich people. Ask people who are new in the neighborhood to come and make them feel at home. Also invite people who might not be able to pay you back. You'll be rewarded for the love you show them.

Do what's just

I love justice, and I expect you to do what's just. Do your part to make sure that laws are fair and that the legal system carries them out in an impartial manner. Work to see that people who are wise and capable of making good decisions are appointed to be judges and other officials.

If you're a judge, be careful to hand down judgments that are just and that help to promote peace. Don't judge a situation or a person by appearances or let someone's financial status influence you. See that all people are treated fairly, regardless of their connections, social position, or the amount of money they have.

Don't take a bribe. It can blind you to the truth and hurt the cause of someone who's seeking justice.

Laws should apply to everyone equally, no matter what color, sex, or religion people are, or whether they're long-time residents or strangers. Remember that you're all equal in my eyes.

How to love other people (43)

A whole family shouldn't be punished for things that a few of its members do, and children shouldn't be punished for things that their parents do. Everyone should be considered responsible for his or her own behavior. 20

A person shouldn't be convicted of a crime unless he or she is given a fair trial and is proved guilty beyond a reasonable doubt. The judge should sentence the person to a punishment that reflects the seriousness of the offense. The punishment should never be more severe than the crime warrants, or the guilty person will end up being treated worse than he or she deserves. 21, 22

Tell the truth

Love, speak, seek, and teach the truth. Don't pass along misleading or untrue reports, falsely accuse or slander anyone, or lie in any way. Don't listen to lies other people tell, either.

If you're involved in a lawsuit, don't give false information, cooperate with someone to be a malicious witness, or let your testimony be swayed by the majority. If you know something about a crime, report whatever you know to the court, even if you're not called to testify. Don't withhold information or the result could be an unjust verdict.

If someone falsely accuses you of doing wrong, go to that person and try to straighten things out peacefully. If this doesn't work, you may want to go before a judge so that the matter can be cleared up as quickly as possible. 23

Don't covet or steal

Be careful not to become so attracted by something that doesn't belong to you that you make plans to take it away from its owner. Don't covet another

person's spouse, home, land, employee, or anything
24 else.

Don't steal from others or in any way deal falsely with them. On the other hand, if someone robs you,
25 forgive him or her.

Be honest in everything you do, even in matters that seem unimportant. You'll then probably be honest about more important matters, too. If you're dishonest in your material dealings, who will ever
26 trust you with friendship and love?

Be a person of integrity in all your business affairs—never take advantage of anyone. For example, use correct measurements of length, weight, and quantity when performing transactions. Don't keep two scales, one accurate and one inaccurate, or
27 conduct business according to two sets of principles.

If you agree to buy or sell something, be sure to pay a fair price or charge a fair price for it. Allow the seller or buyer to change his or her mind during a reasonable period of time. Remember that whatever you have is really mine, and that you're only using it.

Respect the property rights of others. For example, don't tamper with the boundary between your property and your neighbor's. This could cause
28 unnecessary confusion and arguments.

If something you borrow from another person gets damaged while you're using it, you should pay for the damages. Or, if something you own damages something belonging to another person, you should pay for the damages. If you take care of another person's property and something happens to it, be sure to pay for the damages if they were caused by your negligence.

If you've lost something and believe that another person has found it and that person refuses to return it, try to solve the problem between the two of you. If you can't settle your differences in this way, you may need to go before a judge. In any case,
29 settle the matter as quickly as possible.

How to love other people

Don't murder

Don't endanger the life of another person either secretly or openly, or even listen to talk about killing someone else. Do your part to see that people aren't allowed to murder each other under any circumstances. Make sure that a person who's so full of hatred that he or she *deliberately* plans to kill someone else and does it is removed from society. Someone like this is a bad influence in the world.

It's important, however, to safeguard the rights of a person who's killed someone else. For example, the killer must be protected from people who want to avenge the victim's death. He or she should be guaranteed a fair trial; the court, and not avengers of the victim's death, should determine whether or not the killing was done with hatred and premeditation. Any case that's too difficult for local judges to decide should be brought to a higher court.

Try not to harm another person, either deliberately or out of negligence. For example, if you build a house with a flat roof on which people can walk, put a guard rail around the edge of the roof so that no one can fall from it. If you dig a pit for any reason, keep it covered. Do your best not to hurt an animal, either. If you cause a problem for a person or an animal, make amends for it.

If one person deliberately injures another, he or she should pay for the injured person's treatment and loss of time. If there's a difference of opinion, a court, and not the victim or the person who caused the injury, should determine fair compensation.

Choose leaders who keep my agreement

Some leaders take advantage of others while insisting that their actions are for the good of all. Be careful not to choose leaders like these. Instead, support and select leaders who serve the people rather than expect the people to serve them.

Pick leaders who live according to my guidelines, and who read my words regularly. This will prevent them from feeling that they're better than the people they're leading. They'll be less likely to turn away from my agreement, and will probably be good leaders for a long time.

Choose the kind of leaders I myself would choose—men and women who are just and good, who apologize when they do wrong, and who try hard to correct their mistakes. They should be open and honest, and come from your midst rather than being strangers. They shouldn't oppress anyone or use violence to get their way. They shouldn't accumulate money or property for themselves at the expense of others. They should look out for the well-being of the people rather than for themselves.

When you have good leaders, treat them with respect; if you yourself are a leader, be the kind of person I've just described.

Be responsible in sexual relationships and in marriage

I've given you sexual needs, but this doesn't mean that you should feel free to have sexual relations with just anything or anyone. For example, don't have sexual relations with an animal or with someone closely related to you. Don't commit adultery. Use common sense in meeting your sexual needs, and do your best not to hurt yourself or another person. Try not to be influenced by people who are sexually irresponsible.

I encourage you to get married, but not to someone you shouldn't have sexual relations with or to someone who doesn't live according to my guidelines. Choose your partner carefully and wisely. If

How to love other people

you marry, become one with your spouse and establish a home together.

When you're first married, be careful not to assume additional responsibilities that take you away from your spouse. Spend your first year together as freely and happily as possible. No matter how long you're married, though, treat each other with consideration. Don't be unfaithful to your spouse, but rather develop a relationship of friendship, love, and trust with him or her.

Do your best to quickly straighten out any difficulties that may arise between the two of you. If it's absolutely impossible to solve your problems, then you may divorce each other. Keep in mind, however, that I don't like divorce. I want you to take your marriage vows and the marriage vows of others seriously.

Never take advantage of another person sexually, and especially not your spouse. For example, don't force yourself on him or her or anyone else, either, and don't use sex for purely selfish purposes. Do your part to make sure that rapists are punished. A married person who's raped shouldn't be considered guilty of committing adultery, and the marriage shouldn't suffer as a result.

If two people have a child, both of them should help to support the child, whether or not they're married to each other.

Care for your parents and children

Honor your father and your mother, and help any of your relatives who are in need. Show respect toward your elders. When an old person or anyone else dies, however, don't get carried away with mourning for him or her.

When your children are born, they can't tell right from wrong, so you must carefully teach them.

Encourage and guide them to choose what's good and reject what's bad. Tell them about me and the guidelines I've set up for you. If your children ask why they should keep my agreement, explain to them that it's in their best interests to do so. Raise them from an early age to believe that nothing is more important than I am. Never discourage them from following me.

Love your children and tenderly look out for them; treat them as well as I treat you. When you care for them, you're really caring for me. You can learn a lot from your children. An adult who depends on me with the trust and simplicity of a child lives the good life.

Do your best not to take advantage of your children or do anything to harm them. For example, don't try to make a profit from them. Don't have sexual relations with them or influence them to become prostitutes. If you've had two spouses and have had children by both of them, be careful not to give preferential treatment to the children of the spouse you loved more. If your child develops any kind of problem and you can't straighten it out within your family, get help for you, your family, and your child. Make sure that the problem doesn't continue.

Be kind to the people who work for you

Don't treat your employees like slaves. Be kind to them, remembering that each of you is equal in my eyes. Pay them fairly and on time.

If you agree to let people work for you to repay a debt they owe you, don't insist that they work for you the rest of their lives. After a reasonable period of time, free them from any more obligation to you. Don't let them go away empty-handed, however; help them out as much as you can. If they don't

How to love other people

want to leave you, you may continue to employ them.

Don't ever kidnap or sell another person, or keep anyone as a slave. Do your part to see that no one else does, either. If slaves run away from their owners, don't return them; instead, do whatever you can to help them. Never look down on them, but treat them as equals.

If a person marries his or her employee, the employee should be treated as a spouse and not as an employee any longer. If an employer's son or daughter marries an employee, the employee should be accepted as a member of the employer's family.

Being kind to those who work for you is the last of the guidelines that I said I'd spell out for you. They explain how to love me with all your heart, soul, strength, and mind, and others as you love yourself. Follow them and you'll live the good life.

When you're living the good life, you'll want other people to experience it, too. You'll find yourself wanting to talk about me and my agreement. What's the best way to do this? I'll tell you.

V
HOW TO TELL OTHER PEOPLE ABOUT ME

Who my prophets were

1   I love the world I made, and don't like to see anyone who's unhappy or troubled. I feel sorry for people who don't realize that it's in their best interests to live according to the guidelines I've set up. Each and every person is important to me, and I'm sad when even one turns away from me.

2   Because I've always wanted everyone to live the good life, I've looked far and wide for people who were willing to spread the news about me and my agreement. Sometimes I couldn't find anyone. When I did find people who chose to live according to my guidelines and talk about me, I revealed myself to them. I didn't tell them anything they couldn't understand, but instead clearly explained the things I wanted them to know. I helped them to see what would happen if people kept my agreement—and what would happen if they didn't.

My messengers, often called prophets, couldn't keep quiet once they heard what I had to tell them.

How to tell other people about me

Can people who hear an alarm not react to it? Of course not. Neither could my prophets help talking to others about me and my guidelines. Over and over they spoke these words: "Quit doing what's wrong and do what's right instead. Stop serving false gods. Keep God's agreement and you'll live the good life." 3

When people in trouble called out to me, I sent my prophets to them with messages from me. "This is what God wants you to do," they said. Although these people couldn't hear my voice, they could understand my words when they were spoken by ordinary people like themselves.

I often sent my prophets to try to persuade whole nations to follow me. They warned these nations about what would happen to them if they didn't change their ways. Frequently, people stubbornly refused to listen, so the troubles my messengers predicted came true. When people turned to me, however, they avoided the terrible things they'd been warned about. Because my prophets were willing to speak my words, they saved individual people and whole nations alike from disaster. 4

There are people among you today whom I've sent to tell you about me. I want you to listen to them because they speak for me. When you love them, you also love me, so don't stand in their way or make fun of them. 5

Even though I've sent messengers out since I first made people, I'm still asking the question "Who'll tell others about me and my agreement?" Will you answer, "Here I am! Send me!"? 6

Speak my words

If you say the things I tell you to, you'll be my mouth in the world. You'll be responsible for watching over people to see whether they follow me, and for warning them if they don't. 7

If a man agrees to warn people of an approaching army but the people ignore him when he sounds the alarm, it's their fault, not the watchman's fault, if they're taken by surprise. If, on the other hand, the watchman sees the army coming but doesn't sound the alarm, he's responsible if the people are caught off guard.

In the same way, I'm asking you to warn people about what'll happen to them if they break my agreement. If you say that you'll do this, but you don't get around to it, you'll be partially responsible if they don't live the good life.

So tell people about me and admit that you know me. Don't be ashamed of me or deny me. You don't need to shout about me on the street corner, but don't be silent, either. Look for people who'll listen to you. Gather men, women, and even children together and tell them about me.

Boldly speak my words whether people listen to you or not. If I tell you something in the dark, say it in the daylight; if I whisper something to you, speak up about it. Say whatever I tell you to say.

I may ask you to write about me. If I do, write clearly so that people will be able to read your words easily. Write everything I tell you to write.

Remember that people hear what they want to hear. They may not always agree with what you say—but they'll know from your words and actions that you're my messenger.

Go to the world

I want you to do your part to see that every person on earth finds out about me and my agreement. Just as rain makes plants grow, I'd like my words to cause love and justice to flourish thoughout the world. Even though you may not be aware of it, people are waiting to hear about me. Many of them

How to tell other people about me (53)

want to live the good life but don't know how. So don't let them stay in the dark any longer. 14

If workers are sent to straighten out a highway, they'll clear the area, level hills, fill in valleys, and smooth out rough places. Then they'll put up road signs to direct traffic. In the same way, I'm sending you ahead to prepare the way so other people can come to me. Make it as easy as you can for them to find me. 15

Wherever I send you, look for people who are lost, poor, sick, and troubled. Don't waste your time reminding people who already follow me to keep my agreement; concentrate instead on people who haven't yet found me. Healthy people don't need doctors—sick people do. If people are blind to me, 16 help them to see. If they're trapped by their own twisted thinking, help to free them. If they're hungry for me, feed them. Show them how to live the good life. 17

When you bring people to me, they learn to live together in love and peace. By speaking my words and living according to the guidelines I've set up, you're doing your part to make the world a better place. Don't ever do this to get rich, however. I don't 18 charge you when I talk to you, so I don't want you to talk about me in order to make money, either. Spread the news about me because you love others, not because you want to benefit financially. 19

Don't try to get out of doing what I'm asking you to do—and don't try to convince yourself that the time isn't right to tell others about me. Look around you. Can't you see the fields that are ready to be harvested? Someone else sowed them; I'm asking you to reap them. How happy you'll be when you see people living the good life because they've listened to you! 20

Sometimes it may seem as if there are very few people who are willing to labor in the fields! Pray that I'll send others to work with you; in the meantime, though, don't let anything or anyone keep you from telling others about me. Start now!

How can you be sure that I'm the one who's speaking to you and asking you to go out into the world? Here's how: After you've led a person to me and that person learns to keep my agreement, he or she will also want to tell others about me. Where you once worked alone, there'll be two of you working side by side for me.

What to say

Be sure to repeat everything I tell you. Don't hold back a single word. Explain to people that you haven't come to them on your own, but that I've sent you. Tell them that the words you speak aren't yours, but mine. Go on to describe me in such a way that you honor me, not yourself, and people become acquainted with me through you. You may want to illustrate what you say with examples of how I've taken care of you and the love I've shown you.

Point out to people what they're doing wrong, and warn them that they won't live the good life unless they change their ways. When they ask, "Why do terrible things keep happening to us?" answer, "It's because you've been following false gods instead of the true God. You haven't been doing what's good for you; you haven't been living according to God's guidelines."

Teach them the difference between good and bad. Tell them that if they're sorry for the things they've done wrong in the past, make amends for them, and then do what's right, I'll forgive them and give them the good life.

Don't judge people when you're talking to them about me, even if they behave badly. You're on earth to help them, not to condemn them. They'll judge themselves by how they respond to your message from me.

How to tell other people about me

I'll tell you a story to help you understand what I mean by this.

A farmer was sowing grain. Some if it fell along the road, where people walked on it and birds ate it. Some of it fell on rocky ground. It quickly sprouted in the shallow soil, but then the sun scorched it and it withered because it couldn't grow roots. Some seed fell among thorns and was choked when it grew. Other seed fell into fertile soil and produced a crop that was thirty, sixty, and a hundred times more than what the farmer had originally planted.

When you speak my words to people, you're like the farmer sowing grain. Your listeners are like the ground on which the seed falls.

People who hear you but don't understand what you're saying are like the road. The good effects that my words could have on their lives are snatched away from them, just as birds eat seed that falls on the road.

People who accept what you say but don't let it take hold in their lives are like the rocky ground. They keep my agreement for a while, but if they find it at all difficult to follow me, they go back to their old ways.

People who listen to you, but let the cares of the world become more important than my words, are like ground covered with thorns. What I say to them is pushed out of their lives by other things.

People who hear and follow my words are like fertile soil. My words take root in their lives and grow. These kinds of people bring about thirty, sixty, and even a hundred times more good than what was planted in them in the first place.

28

Some people will accept you

Those people who want to know the truth or who already keep my agreement will recognize that your message comes from me. They'll accept you and listen to what you have to say. They'll see you as a bearer of wonderful news, and you'll be beautiful to them.

It's as if you're a vine and the people who believe you are the branches; because I care for the vine, the branches grow strong. I'm the living bread and the living water. When you tell others about me, you give them the bread and water they need to live the good life.

At times you may think that what you say doesn't accomplish anything. That's not true! The effects of my words can be compared to the growth of a tiny mustard seed; it grows into a plant so tall that birds can build nests in its branches. My words affect those who follow them as yeast causes dough to rise; you can't see the yeast, but you can eventually see what it does.

Farmers plant seed without fully understanding how it grows; you spread the news about me in the same way. You may recognize the good results of what you do, but you may not be able fully to understand or control them.

Some people will choose to live according to my guidelines because of your influence. Do your best to see that they keep following me all their lives. Look out for them so that not even one of them turns away from me. Let them know that you always want what's best for them by saying something like this to them:

> May God bless you and watch over you, may God look lovingly upon you, may God be good to you and give you peace.

Be careful not to work against people who live according to my guidelines but don't belong to your particular group—and don't insist that they join your group. After all, there are many different ways of keeping my agreement, and it isn't necessary to combine all of them. You wouldn't use a piece of

How to tell other people about me

unshrunk cloth to patch an old shirt—if you did, the patch would shrink when the shirt was washed and tear the shirt. Just as unshrunk cloth and shrunk cloth shouldn't be put together in a single garment, the different ways of serving me don't need to be joined, either.

People who aren't against you are for you, and those who really follow me won't stand in your way regardless of what group they belong to. Remember this and work side by side with them. On the other hand, people who refuse to live according to my guidelines are against both me and you.

Others will reject you

You'll find that some people you talk to about me won't accept you. They'll be rude, stubborn, and slow to believe anything you say. They'll seem as if they have eyes that don't see and ears that don't hear.

You may illustrate what you say in many different ways, and try your best to get your message across, but some people still won't listen. A few, of course, won't respond to anything. These kinds of people don't dance at weddings or cry at funerals, either. You may try to prove a point by living simply, and some people will say you're crazy. You may eat and drink like anyone else, and others will call you a glutton. Don't worry about people like these.

Some people may tell you that they won't believe anything you say unless you show them a sign or perform a miracle of some kind. I'll tell you a story to help you understand what I mean by this.

There was once a rich man who dressed in purple and fine linen and ate extravagantly every day. A poor man named Lazarus lay at the rich man's doorstep. Lazarus was full of sores that dogs came and licked. He wished that someone would give him the leftovers from the rich man's table. When Lazarus died, the angels carried him to be with Abraham at the feast in heaven. When the rich man died, he was buried and went to hell. There, in torment, he looked up and saw Abraham, far away, with Lazarus at his side.

"Father Abraham," the rich man shouted, "won't you please send Lazarus to dip the end of his finger in water and cool my tongue? I'm in agony!"

"Son," Abraham answered, "remember that in your lifetime you had everything and Lazarus had nothing? Now he's getting what he deserves, and you're getting what you deserve. Besides, there's a great chasm between you and us that no one can cross."

"Then please, Father, send Lazarus to my family," the rich man said. "I want to warn my five brothers so they won't end up here, too."

"Your brothers can listen to the prophets," Abraham answered.

"They won't pay any attention to the prophets, Father," the rich man said. "But they know that Lazarus died, so if he went to them they certainly wouldn't ignore him!"

"If your brothers won't listen to the prophets," Abraham said, "they won't listen to someone who rises from the dead."

In this story, Abraham wouldn't send Lazarus to the rich man's brothers. In the same way, you shouldn't feel pressured by people who want you to perform miracles or give them signs. Instead, tell them about Jonah. He changed from a man who refused to follow me to a man who preached about me to the people of Nineveh. Or tell them about how you've changed since you started living according to my guidelines.

If I send you to people in another country who don't even speak your language, they'll probably listen to you. But if I send you to the people around

How to tell other people about me

you, they may not pay any attention to you at all. Don't let their stubbornness discourage you.

Some people may talk about you behind your back when you speak my words. Others may listen to you and pretend that they believe you without having any intention of doing what you say. They may brag about loving me, but they're really more interested in doing what *they* want than what I want. They may see you as some kind of entertainer, like a person who sings or plays a musical instrument. You may amuse them, but you won't change them.

The types of people I've been describing won't take you seriously. Even though they might accept someone not sent by me, they won't accept you. You may feel like a good shepherd who's rejected by the sheep. Speak my words to them anyway. Point out to them that they're refusing to follow me, not you. Remind them that they're living a lie because they won't accept the truth.

Be careful not to jump to conclusions about people who seem to reject you—or accept you—right away. Sometimes the last to listen are the first to follow, and the first to listen are the last to follow. It doesn't matter because I treat them all the same—whoever keeps my agreement lives the good life. I'll explain what I mean by this.

Very early one morning, a man went out to hire workers for his vineyard. He agreed to pay them the regular wage, and put them to work.

About nine o'clock, he saw some people standing in the marketplace doing nothing. "If you'll work for me," he said to them, "I'll pay you a fair wage." So they agreed to work in the vineyard. At noon, and again at three o'clock in the afternoon, the man hired still more people.

About five o'clock, the man again went to the marketplace and found people idly standing around. "Why aren't you working?" he asked them.

"Because we don't have jobs," they replied.

"You can work in my vineyard," the man said, and they did.

When evening came, the man said to his foreman, "Call all the workers in my vineyard and pay them their wages, beginning with those who started last and ending with those who started first."

The workers who were hired last were each paid the regular rate for a day's work. When the people who were hired first saw this, they were happy because they thought they'd get paid more than the people who were hired last. Instead, they received the same wage. They took their money and started grumbling. "Those who only worked an hour were paid the same as we were. We did a full day's work, and they didn't. It isn't fair!"

The man said to them, "I'm sorry that you're upset, but I didn't mislead you in any way. Didn't you agree with me before you started what the wage would be? It's up to me if I want to pay those who only worked an hour the same as I pay those who worked a full day. I didn't pay you any less because of it. Why do you resent my being generous to others?"

The people who worked in the vineyard were all paid identical wages by the man, regardless of how many hours they'd worked. Like the man, I treat people who keep my agreement as if no one is different from anyone else—I give each of them the good life.

41   I've been explaining how to tell others about me and my agreement. I've said that some people will reject you and may even try to cause trouble for you. You may also run into other problems from time to time because you've chosen to live according to my guidelines. I'll tell you about some of the difficulties you may come up against so you'll be prepared for them and know how to deal with them.

VI
HOW TO COPE WITH TROUBLE

Don't give in to temptation

Be careful not to let anyone or anything influence you to break my agreement. A farmer who tries to plow backward and forward at the same time won't get anywhere; neither can you come closer to living the good life if you keep moving away from me.

The danger of giving in to temptation is always great. That's why you must avoid anything that even seems as if it might cause you to turn away from me. Get rid of the things in your life that keep you from living according to my guidelines. Stay away from anyone who encourages you to quit following me.

You may need to sell something you own if it becomes more important to you than I am. You may even need to cut yourself off from someone you love. You mustn't let anyone or anything take my place in your life.

Sometimes you may feel it's almost impossible to keep living according to my guidelines no matter

(61)

what. It may seem as if you'll have to poke out your own eye because it's influencing you to break my agreement, or cut off your own hand or foot and throw it away. That's how painful it may be to give up something or someone you love. Remember, however, that it's better in the long run to do this than it is to risk losing the good life.

If you let someone influence you to turn away from me, that person becomes a false god to you—and you know what happens then! The false god gets to be a thorn in your side, and you end up being trapped by your own foolishness. You have trouble whichever way you turn.

So even if your parents, spouse, children, and best friend reject me, be careful not to follow in their footsteps. It's all right if people who refuse to live according to my guidelines come to you for help or advice, but you mustn't go to them. Don't make agreements with them, get emotionally involved with them, or rely on them at all. Don't bring anything into your home that tempts you to put it above me, either.

Instead of turning away from me yourself, do whatever you can to help others follow me. If someone tries to get another person to break my agreement, and you hear about it, go to the person who keeps my agreement and give him or her support and encouragement.

When you live according to my guidelines, I bless you with the good life. After you've experienced it for a while, you may be tempted to forget that I'm the one who gave it to you in the first place. Don't let yourself become proud and think that you don't need me anymore. Remember that I'm the one who freed you from your twisted thinking so that you'd be able to keep my agreement. When you went through hard times, I was there to help. The only reason you live the good life is because you follow me.

Be careful not to influence anyone else to quit living according to the guidelines I've set up. You'd be better off if someone tied a weight around your neck and threw you into the sea than if one of my followers broke my agreement because of you. 11

Don't let false prophets influence you

Some people say that they're speaking for me when they really aren't. They claim that I sent them when I didn't. These people, often called false prophets, are liars, and they make me angry! They may fool others, but they can't fool me; I recognize them for what they are. 12 13

Children are supposed to obey their parents, and employees their employers. False prophets say that they're my children and that they do my work in the world, so they should obey me, but they refuse to. They say that I talk to them, but I don't—they wouldn't listen to me if I did. They claim to speak the truth when they don't even know the meaning of the word. 14 15

False prophets may pretend to be concerned about others, but they really care only for themselves. Often, they concentrate on teaching people who can do something for them in return, and ignore everybody else. Instead of living according to my guidelines, false prophets make fun of them. They twist my truths around and change them to suit their own purposes. Sometimes even my own followers get confused by what false prophets say— the words may sound like mine even though they're really not. 16

The power that false prophets have over their listeners is dangerous, and they do a great deal of harm in the world. People who pay attention to them are sadly misled. Their minds get clouded, and their thinking becomes twisted. They may believe that they're following me when they're actually getting further and further away from me all the time. They don't realize that false prophets encourage their listeners to rebel against me, quit keeping my agreement, and forget all about me.

17

People who follow false prophets are trusting in lies. They don't live the good life because the prophets they've chosen to obey have rejected the truth, and they end up rejecting it, too.

18

False prophets are like blind guides. They're like dogs that won't bark at danger, but prefer instead to sleep and dream. They make predictions in my name about the future, but what they're really describing are worthless visions and figments of their own imaginations. Yet they still insist that what they predict will come true!

19

They put useless medicine on people's wounds and claim to be amazed when the wounds won't heal. They fill their listeners with vain hopes by saying, "If you do what I say, everything will be all right. Trust me." They promise the good life to people who don't live according to my guidelines. Everything they say is full of inconsistencies.

20

False prophets are like wolves pretending to be sheep. Just as robbers lie in wait for their victims, false prophets pounce on vulnerable people. They even do their dirty work in churches and synagogues.

21

They're so greedy that they try to profit from the lies they tell about me, and even go so far as to charge people to listen to them. They feed on people's weaknesses. They expect their followers to behave in certain ways while they themselves do whatever they please.

22

Notice how self-indulgent most false prophets are—what they say depends on how comfortable they feel at the moment. When they have plenty to eat, they call for peace, but when they're hungry, they cry for war. They stagger around from drinking

How to cope with trouble

too much and make gluttons of themselves. Everything about them is disgusting and excessive. How can they possibly think that they're capable of guiding others?

23

If these people were really my prophets, wouldn't they live according to my guidelines and encourage others to do the same? Wouldn't they think about someone besides themselves? Of course they would—but they don't. And they get even worse as their numbers increase—the more false prophets there are, the more brazen they all become.

24

You may hear about many false prophets in the world. They'll turn large numbers of people away from me, even including some who've followed me in the past. They may appear to be popular and successful, and have many thousands of followers. Be careful not to be fooled by them yourself.

25

When faced with both false prophets and true prophets, you may find it difficult to tell them apart. I realize that it may be hard for you to know when a prophet is really speaking for me, since false prophets are often very attractive on the surface. So I'll give you ways of testing whether or not a prophet is a follower of mine. Don't go by just one of these ways, though, or you may be misled. Use all of them together and you'll be able to tell a true prophet from a false one.

26

First of all, look to see whether a prophet's predictions come true. My prophets *always* make accurate predictions; false prophets, on the other hand, may or may not. Sooner or later a false prophet is bound to make a mistake.

27

Second, pay attention to how a prophet behaves. True prophets live according to my guidelines; false prophets don't. A thorn bush can't bear grapes and thistles can't produce figs. In the same way, false prophets can't behave as if they're keeping my agreement no matter how hard they try. Their own twisted thinking prevents them from following me. If you watch carefully, you'll see the signs. Remember that people say and do what's in their hearts.

Third, notice whom a prophet praises. True prophets honor me; false prophets talk mainly about themselves. They're more concerned with their own opinions than they are about me.

The final way to tell whether or not a prophet is true is to see if he or she encourages people to live according to my guidelines. True prophets do. False prophets, on the other hand, try to get people to believe in false gods—often including themselves.

I caution you not to be misled by someone simply because he or she can perform miracles. Not everyone who gives signs, cures the sick, or seems to have special powers has been sent by me. For example, some people may practice divination, soothsaying, sorcery, augury, or witchcraft. Don't turn to, seek out, or listen to such people, even if others do. They'll only deceive you. Be careful not to engage in such activities yourself.

Sometimes, a person may say that he or she has come to save the world and claim to be a messiah. If people tell you that they've seen someone like this, or that the messiah will be at a certain place at a certain time, don't believe them. Don't follow them to where they say the messiah is. If you do, you'll be disappointed or misled. Remember that I warned you about this ahead of time.

Straw and wheat aren't the same; neither are false prophets and true prophets. So carefully evaluate the differences between them, as I've told you how to. Point out to false prophets that I haven't sent them and that they're causing people to trust in lies. Do your part to get rid of the false prophets in the world.

Be careful never to be a false prophet yourself. When I tell you something, speak my words without changing them. Don't add to or subtract from them, or use them to suit your own purposes instead of mine. If you're going to be my messenger in the world, do it right. 34

Don't turn away from me if you're persecuted

When you live according to my guidelines, you're different from people who don't, and it shows. You get to be more and more like me every day. People who reject me may find you a disturbing influence in their lives. 35

If you were like the people who refuse to keep my agreement, or went along with their ideas, they'd probably love you for it. But because you're different from them, they might see you as a threat and try to make trouble for you. At times, you may feel like a sheep surrounded by wolves. 36, 37

Keep in mind that people who reject me will also reject you for following me. Instead of respecting you because you live according to my guidelines, they'll look down on you and do their best to harm your reputation. They'll speak of you with contempt, and stand in your way at every turn. They may even force you to work for them and their leaders. 38

Whenever you talk about me, you run the risk of angering those who refuse to follow me. Even though you bring a message of peace and love, your words may cause conflict and dissension. Your message from me may split families and communities apart. Father may turn against son, and son against father; mother may turn against daughter, and daughter against mother. A family of five may be divided three against two and two against three. It may seem at times as if you're setting the world on fire. 39, 40

If you try to tell your friends and relatives about me, you may find that they're your worst enemies.

They may ridicule you or tell you to mind your own business. Your brothers, sisters, parents, and others you love may even turn against you and fight you with everything they have. Remember the old saying that prophets are honored everywhere but in their own home towns and among their own families.

Sometimes even people who believe the things you say won't be there when you need them. They may deny that they ever had anything to do with you if they're threatened or persecuted because of their relationship with you. Although they may have promised to die for you if necessary, they'll abandon you as surely as sheep scatter when the shepherd is injured.

Some people may call you a liar when you claim that you speak for me. Others may say that you're crazy and leave it at that. My prophets have been made fun of and harassed down through the centuries, so try not to be upset about this.

Some people may accuse you of being a bad influence in the world. How ridiculous! They should open their eyes and see the good things you do because you're living according to my guidelines. A house divided against itself can't stand—and neither would you be able to do what's good if you were as bad as these people say you are.

Some people may consider you dangerous and want to get you out of circulation as quickly as possible. They may bring charges against you, take you to court, and try to have you convicted of a crime, hoping that you'll be put away. If you end up in front of a judge, look upon it as an opportunity to talk about me.

Some people may harm you physically. They may beat you in their churches and synagogues, and wound you so badly that you feel as if you no longer look like yourself. You'll learn about grief and sorrow first hand. It may even seem that I've turned against you, too—but I haven't.

Some people may want to kill you, just as their

ancestors killed my prophets of old. They may convince themselves that by killing you they're serving me. They may plan to bury you like a common criminal, or hold a magnificent funeral for you if it suits their purposes.

No matter how badly you're persecuted, however, be careful not to quit keeping my agreement. Remember that I put you on earth to be a living example of my words so that others would take them seriously. The world needs to see someone who lives according to my guidelines regardless of what happens to him or her. I'll explain why this is so important.

When people try to hurt you for following me, you're in a sense taking the bad things they've done upon yourself. You're suffering because of what *they've* done, not because of anything *you've* done. If you keep living according to my guidelines without wavering in the least, even though other people mistreat you or do everything they can to change your mind, you'll prove something to them. Your words and actions may even cause some of them to regret the way they've been behaving and decide to follow me instead.

Your suffering, then, may bring people to me. Because of you, they'll live the good life. It's as if you offer yourself as a ransom for them—you're like a lamb that's sacrificed in place of a person who's about to be executed.

This may be very difficult for you to understand. You may be wondering why you should have to go through all these problems for the sake of people you may not even know. It may seem a lot easier just to forget all about me than to put up with persecution. Keep in mind, though, that some of the same people who make trouble for you may turn to me later because of you. How awful it would be if you just ran away and left all of them to die without ever knowing me!

Unless a grain of wheat falls into the ground and

dies, it can't grow and bear fruit. Like the grain, you must be willing to die for me if you're going to do my work in the world. The greatest love you can show
49 another person is to give your life for him or her.

Remember when I first told you about what it means to live according to my guidelines? I said then that I'd never force you to follow me, and that it would always be up to you. So it's up to you to decide whether or not you'll go along with being persecuted during your lifetime. Keep in mind, though, that when you live according to the guidelines I've set up, things are right between you and me; you're at peace with yourself and with me. You can't find this peace in any other way. It's true that you help others by allowing yourself to be mistreated because of me, and that's important. But what's even *more* important is the peace of mind you have as a result of following me. That's worth much more than anything you could ever gain by turning away from me for whatever reason.

If you choose to keep following me regardless of what other people do to you, I'll be with you at all times and give you life that lasts forever. What good would it do if you gained the whole world and lost life that lasts forever? What good would it do if you turned away from me at the expense of your own peace of mind? No matter how powerful your persecutors may seem—and no matter how many of them there are—you'll have something that they don't have: a good relationship with me, and all the bene-
50 fits that go with it.

So do whatever's necessary to keep my agreement all your days, and you won't regret it. Live according to my will, not yours. This is what I'm
51 asking you to do.

When people force you to leave one town because they don't like the fact that you follow me, hold your head up and go on to the next. Foxes have holes and birds have nests, but there may be times

How to cope with trouble

when you don't have a place to call your own. Don't let this get you down, though; look on it as an opportunity to spread the news about me from place to place. In this way, people from one end of the earth to the other will have the chance to find out about me. 52

Wherever you're forced to go, don't spend your time and energy regretting the things you left behind. Start a new life. Build a house and live in it. Plant a garden. Raise your family. Then see that your children marry and have children of their own. Teach them about me, too. Work for the good of whatever country you're living in, and you'll benefit as well. 53

Don't be afraid of people who persecute you for my sake, even though they do their best to harm you. Don't let anything they say or do upset you. Remember that I'm much greater than they are. 54 Learn to live with persecution if you must. Don't spend your life complaining. Forgive the people who make trouble for you; they don't really know what they're doing. 55

Instead of feeling sorry for yourself, be happy in spite of the fact that people make fun of you, tell lies about you, and reject you because of me. Their ancestors treated my prophets of old in the same way. It would actually be far worse for you if these people spoke well of you. They're the type who'd support false prophets, so you certainly don't need their approval. 56

Keep watch over yourself!

I've been explaining the kinds of trouble you may come up against when you choose to live according to my guidelines. You'll probably run across temptation, false prophets, and persecution in one form or another. Any or all of these could cause you to turn away from me if you aren't careful.

During especially bad times, many people may quit following me and end up rejecting me altogether. They'll stop loving themselves and turn against one another. The messengers I send to help 57 them may not be able to find anyone willing to listen. I'm telling you this ahead of time so that you won't be influenced to turn away from me, too. I don't want you to break my agreement regardless of what 58 goes on around you.

Be sure that you don't forget any of the things 59 I've told you so you won't get confused or be misled. Take all of my words to heart and meditate on them day and night. If there seems to be a contradiction between what I say and what you think is right, do what I say. Apply my words to every situation you encounter, every thought you have. I want them to 60 be a part of your life.

Think about how I've helped people in the past. A careful homemaker uses both old and new supplies from the storeroom. In the same way, try to remember the lessons you've learned and also add to them 61 the knowledge you're gaining every day.

Pray that I'll give you the strength to face temptation without yielding to it. Temptation can be very appealing—that's why it's dangerous. There may be times when your mind says one thing about following 62 me and your body says another.

When you least expect it, you may have to answer for your words and deeds. Don't think for a minute that just because you can get away with something for a while you won't be held responsible for it eventually. Sooner or later, every person on earth will bear the consequences of his or her own 63 behavior.

So do what's right at all times; that means keeping my agreement constantly. Don't let yourself get sidetracked by anyone or anything. If people know ahead of time when thieves will arrive, they can be ready for them and keep them from breaking in; because you don't know when you'll have to account for your behavior, you must stay on your toes all the time. 64

For example, if a man tells his servants that he plans to be out late, and asks them to stay up for him so that they can open the door when he knocks, the good servants stay awake all night if they have to. When the man does return home, he's so happy to see his servants waiting for him that he takes off his coat, asks his servants to sit at the table, and serves them himself. He rewards them because they're prepared for him. 65

Here's another example of what I mean.

A man was going out of town, so he put his employees in charge of his business. He told each of them what he expected him or her to do while he was gone. He didn't tell them precisely what day he'd be back, but he did warn them that he didn't want to find them sleeping on the job when he returned.

Some of the employees did what the man told them to do. Others waited until they were sure that he'd gone and then said to one another, "He won't be back for quite a while; we can do whatever we please in the meantime." They started wasting time and abusing the other employees.

The man came back when his employees least expected him, and found the bad ones fooling around at his expense. Naturally, he was angry with them. The good employees, however, had done exactly what the man had told them to do. The man could have come back at any time and found them ready for him. The man knew this, and rewarded them for their good behavior.

You know what's expected of you, so you have no excuse for not doing it. Keep a careful watch over yourself so you're as ready to answer for your words and deeds as the good employees were. I'll reward you, just as the employer rewarded his good employees.

Here's another story to help you understand what I'm talking about.

Ten bridesmaids each took an oil lamp and went out to meet the bridegroom. Five of them were foolish; five of them were wise. The foolish bridesmaids didn't take any extra oil with them, but the wise bridesmaids did.

The bridegroom was late, and the women fell asleep while they were waiting. At midnight, they were suddenly awakened by someone shouting, "Here comes the bridegroom! Come and meet him!" The ten women jumped up and started trimming their lamps.

"Give us some of your oil," the foolish bridesmaids said to the wise ones. "Our lamps are going out."

"We don't have enough oil for both you and us," the wise bridesmaids answered. "You'll have to go and get some."

The five foolish bridesmaids went to get oil. While they were gone, the bridegroom came. He and the five wise bridesmaids went in to the marriage feast. They closed the door behind them and locked it.

The foolish bridesmaids finally came back and knocked on the door. "Open up!" they cried.

"I don't know who you are," the bridegroom said, and refused to open the door.

The wise bridesmaids weren't sure when the bridegroom would come, but they were ready for him anyway. Like them, you must take care not to quit living according to my guidelines even for a moment. Be as prepared to give an account of your behavior as the wise bridesmaids were to meet the bridegroom.

I've been explaining that you must learn to cope

with trouble in order to live the good life. It's in your own best interests to listen to me. Just in case you're not convinced, however, I'll explain what can happen to you if you don't keep my agreement.

68

VII
WHAT HAPPENS IF YOU BREAK MY AGREEMENT?

Your thinking gets twisted

In order to live the good life, you must carefully keep my agreement. Don't ever add to or subtract from anything I've told you, or turn to the right or left to avoid doing something you know you should do. I've spelled out my guidelines for you, so you shouldn't have any doubts or questions about what it means to follow me.

Even though you choose to keep my agreement, you may find yourself turning away from me for one reason or another from time to time. If this happens, and if you come back to me, I forgive you, and things are right between us again. If, on the other hand, you keep doing wrong over and over without being sorry for it, you start to change. You gradually become a different person than you would be if you were living according to my guidelines. This is a serious matter, and I want you to understand just how serious it is. So I'll explain in detail what can happen to you if you reject me.

What happens if you break my agreement? (77)

When you live according to my guidelines, you do what's right and avoid doing what's wrong. You live openly, and you're not ashamed of your words or deeds. If you start to do bad things more and more often without making amends for them, however, you try to hide these things from me and from the people around you—and even from yourself. You're no longer the open type of person you used to be.

If you don't come back to me right away, you begin rationalizing your behavior by telling yourself that you really aren't doing anything all that bad. You even lie when necessary to mislead others. You say that you love me, but you're not as serious about it as you used to be. You claim to enjoy following me, but you no longer mean what you say. You go to church or temple and pray beautiful prayers to me, asking that my will be done, but your mind wanders. You think more about what you want than what I want. You're fast becoming a hypocrite—and you know how I feel about hypocrites!

Imagine that you have two sons. You go to the older and say, "Son, I want you to do some work for me today," and he does what you tell him to do. Then you call your younger son to you and say, "Son, I need your help today."

"Sure, anything you want," he says, and then he goes out and does something else.

When you say that you live according to my guidelines and you do, you're like the older son; when you say that you're keeping my agreement but you really aren't, you're a hypocrite like the younger son. If you no longer follow me, it means that you no longer love me, whether you say you do or not—it's as simple as that.

You may feel a little guilty about what's happening between you and me. If you don't make things right with me, though, you may tell yourself, "God's with me and has always been my friend. If I do something wrong, God'll understand and won't get angry with me." You may even convince yourself that you have a special relationship with me because someone close to you does. If your spouse, your parent, your child, or your friend loves me and follows me, you may start believing that he or she can keep my agreement for you.

Since you're living according to my guidelines less and less, you cause problems for yourself. If you don't admit this, you start putting the blame on others for your difficulties. You may even ask me to punish them. "Give them what they deserve, God," you may say. "After all, it's their fault that I'm not following you as closely as I used to. If they weren't making all this trouble for me, I'd have more time for you."

The less attention you pay to me, the more likely you are to be fooled by false prophets—they usually say the kinds of things you want to hear. For example, I've told you to honor your parents and care for them whenever they're in need. False prophets may say that it's more important to give your money to me—or, in other words, to them—than it is to help your parents out. They ignore the fact that giving to your needy parents is the same as giving to me.

False prophets substitute their own words for mine—and you believe them because you *want* to believe them. You learn their teachings as carefully as you used to learn mine. You convince yourself that false prophets are really speaking for me.

Under their influence, you learn religious rituals that are supposed to please me. You even make up some of your own. Now, when you have problems, you think that it's because you haven't been performing these rituals correctly. You think that rituals will bring you closer to me, but they won't. Why? Because I never asked you to do them in the first place. What I want you to do is to love me and other people—and rituals have nothing to do with this.

What happens if you break my agreement?

Rituals are actually very dangerous because they can give you a false sense of confidence about your relationship with me. Doing them can make you feel as if you're closer to me than you really are and better than the people who don't perform rituals. How ridiculous! Rituals are no substitute for living according to my guidelines, and they certainly can't make up for the bad things you say and do. 9

The fact that things aren't right between you and me may bother you more and more. Instead of coming back to me, however, you may try to ease your conscience in other ways. For example, you may help to build a new house of worship for me, thinking that this will cover up for your bad behavior. You may contribute large sums of money to your church or temple—but for the wrong reasons. When you attend services in these buildings, you're there under false pretenses. 10

In addition to blaming others for your problems, you start criticizing me. "Things didn't go well for me today, God," you may say, "because you didn't look out for me. Where were you when I needed you?" When I don't seem to respond to you, you 11 deliberately and openly disregard my guidelines, and then you dare me to punish you. You don't even bother to try to hide your bad behavior anymore. 12

You no longer enjoy hearing my words. You brush my messengers aside by saying, "They're just a bunch of windbags who don't know what they're talking about. I hope that the terrible things they predict happen to them! God doesn't care about what I do—that's obvious—so I can do whatever I please." You convince yourself that the only way to 13 get ahead in the world is to walk all over other people. "I have to look out for myself," you say, "or people will take advantage of me. It's better to hurt them before they can hurt me." 14

You may not know it, but a great hatred is growing within you. Even though you may still pretend that you care for others, you really despise them. You no longer love me, and you don't even like yourself. My messengers try to help you, but you don't want to hear what they're saying. You claim that they're crazy and do whatever you can to shut them up. You no longer know me—and you don't care.

You've twisted things around so much in your own mind that you insist that you're right and the rest of the world is wrong. You think that what's bad is really good and what's good is really bad. You look down on the people who do follow me and make fun of them. If I myself were to come to you, you'd probably mock me.

You can't see how much you've changed and how you're hurting yourself. You don't realize that your thinking fills your whole being just as a light fills a room. If your thinking were good, goodness would spread throughout you, but it can't when your thinking is twisted.

Finally, you reach the point where you couldn't do good even if you tried. Leopards can't change their spots, and people can't change the color of their skin; neither are you capable of changing what you've let yourself become. Unless you return to me, you stay a prisoner of your own twisted thinking.

I reject you

Even when you deliberately cut yourself off from me, I still want to help you, but I can't as long as you refuse to come back to me. After a while, I get tired of waiting for you, and I no longer feel sorry for you.

When you don't love me anymore, you don't deserve to have the special relationship with me that you had while you were following me. So I quit planning for your future, and I no longer treat you kindly. When you're in trouble and pray to me, I

What happens if you break my agreement?

don't answer you. Even though you call me again and again, shout for me, cry out loud, go without eating, make me offerings, or promise to give up something for me, I don't listen to you. You were once my child, but you've become a stranger to me. It's as if you've allowed someone to put a hook in your nose and a bit in your mouth and lead you further and further away from me and the good life.

24, 25

26

I'll tell you a story to help you understand what I mean.

A man decided to put a vineyard on a fertile hill. He and his gardener plowed the land, picked up all the rocks, and planted the best vines they could buy. When harvest time came, however, they were disappointed. The only grapes that had grown were so bad that they were inedible.

This happened for three years in a row. Finally, the man said to his gardener, "I've waited long enough for good grapes, and I don't want to bother with this vineyard anymore. Pull up the vines and throw them away."

"Let's give them one more year," the gardener suggested. "We'll pay special attention to them and put lots of fertilizer around them. If they bear good grapes next year, the extra work will have been worth it. If not, we can get rid of them then."

So the man and his gardener worked hard to dig up the bad roots in the vineyard. They cut down wild vines and those with withered leaves, and carefully pruned the rest. In spite of all their hard work, though, the vines didn't bear good grapes. Because of this, the man and his gardener took down the fence around the vineyard. They let animals trample and eat the vines. The former vineyard became a wasteland.

Whose fault was it that the vines didn't bear good fruit? Was either the man or the gardener responsible? Of course not. They did everything they could for the vineyard.

You're like a vineyard that I've planted with

choice vines. When you refuse to keep my agreement in spite of everything I do for you, I no longer take care of you. You deteriorate, just as the abandoned vineyard did.

Here's another story that will help you to understand what happens to you when you reject me.

A baby girl was left in an open field to die. The king heard about her and went out to look for her. He was happy when he found her, and made arrangements for someone to take care of her.

The girl grew up and became a prostitute. In spite of this, the king married her and made her his queen. He bought her the finest clothes, gave her expensive jewelry, and put a crown on her head. Because the king treated her so well, the queen grew very lovely. She was so beautiful that people everywhere heard about her.

When she was first married, the queen loved her husband and had children with him. Soon, however, she started thinking that she could get along without the king. She forgot that he had saved her life and that she was queen because of him. She stopped loving him, and started being unfaithful to him. She slept with anyone she pleased—soldiers, governors, and commanders, all of them desirable young men.

After a while, the queen grew tired of the men around her. She fell in love with pictures of handsome men who lived in faraway countries. She invited them to come and see her, and they did. She bathed herself for them, and used what the king had given her—her clothes, her jewels, and her food—to please them.

After her lovers had slept with her, the queen no longer cared for them and turned away from them in disgust. Soon, she was sleeping with anyone. Nothing could stop her; anyone who wanted her could have her.

The king begged the queen to quit running after other lovers. "You wear shoes to protect your feet," he said to her. "You drink water when you're thirsty.

What happens if you break my agreement? (83)

Yet you don't have enough sense to come back to me, your loving husband. You're not even ashamed of the way you're acting!"

"I can't help myself," the queen replied. "I like to sleep with anyone I can, and I'm going to keep doing it."

The queen took the children she had had with the king and let her lovers sleep with them, too. Then she had the nerve to speak ill of the king in front of his friends.

She built a brothel on a street corner and offered herself to anyone who passed by. After a while, she began to refuse payment for her services. Instead, she bribed people to become her lovers. She sat alone by the roadside waiting for them.

Finally the king gave up on the queen and divorced her. He took away all the good things he'd given her. When her lovers saw this happening, they turned against her, too. They robbed her of everything she had left, and laughed in her face. Then they went away and forgot all about her.

The queen used to make fun of the people around her, and now everyone made fun of her. She had nowhere to turn. In desperation, she pulled out her own hair and tore at her clothes. Yet she still refused to apologize to the king. The king vowed that he wouldn't ever have anything to do with her again until she stopped being unfaithful and came back to him. He let it be known that if she returned to him, he'd forgive her and treat her as if nothing had ever happened. He waited and waited for her.

This story may seem exaggerated and extreme, but stop for a minute and think about it. When you turn away from me, you're as foolish as the queen was. When you misuse the good things I've given you with no regard for me, you act as she did. When you care for other things more than you do for me, it's as if you're prostituting yourself. I keep waiting for you to change your mind and come back to me.

28

Like the king, I refuse to put up with your

29, behavior. I no longer protect you or take care of you.
30, The things you love more than me end up destroying
31, you. Unless you make things right with me, I won't
32 have anything to do with you.

You get confused and distressed

The more you reject me, the more you cut yourself off from the good life. Although you may realize that things aren't going well for you, your thinking has become so twisted that you don't know
33 what to do. Even donkeys and cattle have enough sense to stay with the people who take care of them, but you're so confused that you no longer know the difference between what helps you and what hurts
34 you.

When I offer you the good life, you won't take it. It's as if you've made up your mind to keep on hurting yourself. You're like a baby who refuses to be
35 born when its mother goes into labor.

Your biggest mistake is in thinking that you
36 know more than I do. You stiffen your neck, turn a stubborn shoulder, plug your ears, and close your eyes to what's good for you. You don't realize how much your own behavior is sapping your strength
37 and aging you.

When people fall down, they get up. When they take the wrong road by mistake, they return to the right road as soon as they can. They use common sense. But you fall down and refuse to get up; you take the wrong road and don't even try to find the
38, right one. You're like a sheep that strays from the
39 shepherd and wanders around lost; you're like someone who walks about aimlessly in the dark without
40 knowing where he or she is going.

You reach the point where my guidelines seem monotonous and repetitious to you—and you don't want anything to do with them. You can't see how much simpler it would be to live by them than to try

What happens if you break my agreement? (85)

to get around them. If you hadn't ever heard about me, nobody would blame you for not knowing enough to follow me. But you know about me, yet you refuse to keep my agreement. That shows how foolish you've become.

You desperately want to be happy, but you feel miserable. You long for peace of mind, but you're not willing to take the steps necessary to find it. Instead of being calm, you're like the waves that toss on a stormy sea.

Your worst fears come true—and then some. The sound of a leaf blowing in the wind terrifies you. You feel as if someone is chasing you all the time. In the morning, you say, "If only it were evening!" At night you lie in bed and wish, "If only it were morning!" You're as frightened as a sheep that knows it's being hunted by lions, or a person who's trapped in a hole. It's as if you manage to get out of one mess only to find yourself in another, or flee into the safety of your own home only to be bitten by a poisonous snake waiting there. Everything seems hopeless. You feel as if you're all alone in the world, and can't think of a single person who really cares about you.

Because you're so disturbed, you become physically ill. Although you take all kinds of medicine, nothing can cure you. You may get to the point where you can't even cry anymore. You feel numb. You no longer enjoy living, and you often wish you were dead.

You're good for nothing

By this time, happiness and love have gone out of your life. You spend your time and energy in useless ways. It seems as if you can't do anything right anymore. Everything you touch is cursed, no matter where you go or what you try to do. Nothing satisfies you.

Just as birds fly away from the nest, your children leave you. Your heart breaks with longing for them, but they never return. You try to find someone to take their place, but you can't. Once, you may have had as many relatives as stars in the sky, but even they disappear like morning mist or smoke rising out of a chimney. Finally, there's no one left to carry on your family name.

When you try to save money, you can't; you may as well carry it around in a bag with no bottom. Your business fails, and financial ruin comes when you least expect it and are least prepared for it.

You seem to be getting smaller and smaller all the time. The good reputation you had in the past disappears. People you once trusted reject and ridicule you. No one feels sorry for you, comforts you, or helps you. No one even bothers to ask how you are.

It's as if your sun has gone down forever. You're so ashamed of your situation that you don't dare show your face. You're good for nothing, as useless as a broken pot. My followers see you as an example of how *not* to behave. When their children ask, "How could God let someone be so unhappy?" they answer, "It's not God's fault. People who refuse to live according to God's guidelines bring trouble on themselves."

There's no hope for you

I don't like to see what's happening to you, and it hurts me to have to treat you like a stranger. I hold out my arms to you one more time and plead, "I'm here. Come to me." But if you don't make things right with me, you rebel against me even more.

You still can't see why you're suffering. You still don't understand that I'm the only one who can help you. You bring worse problems on yourself, but it doesn't seem to make any difference to you. You

What happens if you break my agreement?

won't come back to me regardless of what happens to you.

Imagine that a silversmith puts what he thinks is a piece of silver into a smelter to remove its impurities. The fire burns fiercely and the metal melts, but the impurities remain. What he thought was silver turns out to be a piece of worthless metal, so he doesn't bother with it any longer. If someone tries to clean a rusty pot and finds that nothing can remove the rust, he or she throws the pot away. I feel the same about you when you won't learn from your mistakes.

Finally, you may reach the point where you totally close your mind to me, and I can no longer do anything for you. Like a high wall with a crack in it that suddenly crashes to the ground and can't be repaired, you're beyond hope. By continually refusing to return to me, you inflict an incurable wound on yourself, and nothing can help you. Even if people who follow me pleaded with me to save you from yourself, I wouldn't listen to them.

Although I once loved you and took care of you, you've changed so much that I can no longer bear to have you near me. I don't even come to you and make things easier for you when you die, so your death is terrible. The people who hear about it are horrified, and hope that they'll never have to experience anything like it.

A rotten vine is useless; not even the wood in its branches is worth anything—it might as well be thrown away and burned. Instead of taking you to be with me when you die, I throw you away as if you were a rotten vine. It hurts me to have to do this, but I want nothing more to do with you ever again.

I've told you about what can happen to you if you reject me because I want you to understand how awful it can be for you. When you stop following my guidelines, you lose both the good life and life that lasts forever. Nothing in the world is worth this much of a sacrifice. So take my words to heart, and use them to give you strength when you're tempted to turn away from me even for a minute. Carefully keep my agreement all your days and none of the things I've described will happen to you.

When you turn away from me, not only do you hurt yourself, you're also a bad influence in the world. If everyone refused to live according to my guidelines and became unhappy and hateful, the world would be a hell on earth. I'll explain what I mean by this.

VIII
WHAT HELL ON EARTH WOULD BE LIKE

People reject me

I've been telling you how terrible it can be for you if you turn away from me and stop living according to my guidelines. Not only do you lose the good life, but you also influence the people around you to reject me. If many people refused to keep my agreement, the world would become a hell on earth filled with unhappiness, hatred, and fear—the opposite of what I want it to be.

Of course, this couldn't occur overnight. It might happen so gradually that you wouldn't even realize how bad things were getting until it was almost too late. I'll describe how the world could become a hell on earth because I want you to be able to recognize the signs and do your best to stop this from taking place.

When people start worshiping false gods instead of keeping my agreement, they take the first step toward making the world a hell on earth. They encourage their own sons and daughters to ignore me, and the children follow in their parents' footsteps. Then they all fall madly in love with their false gods and forget about me. The more they prosper, the more they're convinced that these gods are responsible for their success. They don't realize that I'm the one who gives them everything they have, not their false gods.

These people don't see how foolish it is to worship anyone or anything but me—whether it's an image, another person, an object, or an idea that takes my place in their minds. Rather than living the good life by following me, they give it up by choosing to put their time and energy into serving false gods.

When people decide to worship false gods, it's because they aren't thinking clearly. If they were, they'd recognize that I'm the only true God and that they should come back to me for their own good. It's hard for me to believe that people would turn away from me and put their faith in lies. Do they think that I'm too old or tired to know what's going on? Do they tell themselves that I'm dead, or that I never even existed?

After people start believing in false gods, it's easy for them to be fooled by sorcerers, mediums, wizards, and others like them. Some people start spending their nights in graveyards or shrines, hoping to receive messages from the dead. Others watch the sun, moon, and stars for signs that they believe can tell them how to live. They look everywhere but to me. How ridiculous!

Even some of my own messengers stop living according to my guidelines and turn into false prophets. They start telling lies about me and misleading their listeners. Soon they stir up so much trouble that people who really want to follow me get confused.

Instead of watching over people and teaching them how to keep my agreement, false prophets trick

What hell on earth would be like (91)

them with their smooth words. They say, "Let's not talk about right and wrong anymore. Let's discuss how to get ahead in the world." They don't explain how important it is for people to live according to my guidelines. They actually encourage people to do bad rather than good, but do it so subtly that their listeners don't realize what's happening.   10

False prophets behave as if they're in a deep sleep. Nobody is as blind or deaf as they are—they have eyes, but they don't see; they have ears, but they don't listen. To them, the good life is like a closed book. If someone were to hand them the book, they'd say, "I can't read it because it isn't open." But even if someone were to open the book and then hand it back to them, they'd say, "I still can't read it."   11

People begin to listen to prophets who only tell them what they want to hear. They lose interest in my words; they'd rather be entertained by pretty stories. "Don't be so serious all the time," they say to my messengers. "Talk about something besides God." If someone were to go to these people and say, "Today I'm going to preach about the joys of getting drunk," they'd crowd around to listen.   12, 13

People mistreat my followers

In a world that's becoming a hell on earth, my messengers try to warn people against serving false gods and false prophets, but they find fewer and fewer listeners. Many people who once faithfully kept my agreement turn against me and never come back to me again. They may pretend to follow me, and even pray to me from time to time when they want something, but they're hypocrites. Soon, they ignore me altogether.

More and more people spend their whole lives disregarding me. They refuse to accept criticism or guidance from anyone, and when they do something wrong they don't apologize or make amends for it. They have enough energy to do whatever they want, but claim that it takes too much effort to live according to my guidelines. My messengers get frustrated when they can't find anyone who'll listen to them. "Maybe we're talking to the wrong people," they say. Regardless of where they go or what they do, most people refuse to take them seriously.

Instead, people start complaining about my followers. "Who do they think they are to talk to us like this?" they ask each other. "After all, we're not children. Why do they keep telling us the same things over and over again? Do they think we're stupid?" They make trouble for my messengers, and nobody stops them. They even murder them and get away with it until the world is starving—not for food, but for my words. Fewer and fewer people live according to my guidelines, and those who do are persecuted for choosing to follow me. This makes me very angry.

I'll tell you a story to help you understand how I feel about people who mistreat my followers.

A man planted a vineyard and put a wall around it. He furnished all the equipment necessary to produce a good crop, and made sure that everything was in order. Then he rented it to people who promised to take care of it and pay him after the harvest.

When it was time, the man sent one of his employees to collect the rent. But the tenants abused the employee and sent him away empty-handed.

The man sent another employee, and the tenants beat him severely. When a third employee attempted to collect the rent, the tenants killed him.

The man kept sending employees to his tenants, and each one was rejected or harmed. Finally, he sent his own son, thinking, "Surely, they'll respect him!"

The tenants saw the owner's son approaching,

What hell on earth would be like (93)

and said to one another, "Here comes the heir to the vineyard. If we kill him, too, the vineyard will be ours!" So they took the owner's son, murdered him, and threw his body out of the vineyard. **21**

You can imagine how furious the owner was when he heard about this. I, too, am angry when **22** people persecute my followers. People may fool themselves into believing that they can get away with doing wrong, but they're mistaken. **23**

People aren't ashamed when they do wrong

People who choose to follow false gods and false prophets for a long time finally reach the point where they're not ashamed of anything they do. They actually enjoy doing wrong and don't regret it in the least. They even brag about their bad behavior, and **24,** go out of their way to show how little they love me **25** and those around them.

Rather than trying to help one another, these people lie awake all night plotting and scheming against each other. When morning comes, they can't wait to get up and carry out the plans they made the night before. **26**

They start lawsuits to do mischief instead of solving problems; they lie under oath; they're biased and unfair. They undermine honest witnesses and judges, and do anything they can to confuse them.

Even many judges aren't honest. They take bribes and convict innocent people; they write bad laws; they let the word of a single witness be sufficient evidence for sending someone to jail. They take advantage of the poor, and fill their own homes with things that don't belong to them. **27**

The rich get richer, and the poor get poorer. The rich become so greedy that they're never satisfied, while the poor are lucky if they have a decent place to sleep. Some rich people are lazy and expect to be waited on constantly; others spend all their time boasting about how wealthy they are. They brag about how they earned everything they have. Some even say, "Thank God I'm rich!" when they know very well that I'm not responsible for their wealth. They never stop to consider what happens to people who get rich at the expense of others—sooner or later, they lose everything.

Then there are the pleasure-seekers who drink all day long and congratulate themselves on how much liquor they can consume. Others load their tables with food and eat themselves sick. "Bring more!" they holler. They love to listen to background music while they eat, but never give a thought to me.

More and more people don't care if they hurt others. They force poor people to work for them and then cheat them out of their wages. They don't feed the hungry or give drink to the thirsty; they don't welcome strangers, and they refuse to visit those who are sick or in prison. Instead, they walk all over anyone they can. They pretend to be friendly to their neighbors while planning how to take advantage of them. Eventually, no one can trust anyone else—not even members of the same families.

Business people become unprincipled and do anything they can to deceive their customers. They charge the poor high prices for inferior goods, and the poor stay poor all their lives. If people decide that they want things that belong to other people, they take them. Even in broad daylight, they break into one another's homes or rob each other on the streets. Lenders charge too much interest, and borrowers do whatever they can to get out of paying back what they owe.

It seems as if people can't be trusted to tell the truth anymore. They make up stories about each other until no one knows what to believe. Promises and agreements are meaningless because few people honor them.

What hell on earth would be like (95)

Men and women engage in all kinds of sexual misconduct, and openly commit adultery and incest. They don't bother to keep themselves clean, and live in unsanitary surroundings. They eat unhealthy food and make little effort to control the spread of disease.

Parents care only about themselves and neglect their children. The children grow up doing whatever they want and going wherever they want, and eventually turn on their parents; when they themselves get older, their own children turn on them.

People everywhere are so angry with themselves and one another that they get violent. Crime spreads, and murder follows murder. People hunt down their own relatives until no one is safe. Those who are in power kill again and again without regret or feeling.

In spite of what's happening to the world, people go on with business as usual. They eat, drink, marry one another, buy, sell, plant, and build without stopping to figure out why the world is full of so much trouble.

33

34

35

36

37

People choose bad leaders

Because people don't come back to me, they fall into the hands of leaders who openly rebel against me. Instead of doing what's best for the people, these leaders do whatever they want. They're inexperienced and unwise. Some of them spend their time partying, while others associate with people who mock them and know what fools they are. They choose stupid advisers who are so confused that they're incapable of counseling anyone. The advisers give bad advice, and the people and their leaders believe in them and trust them.

These leaders don't apologize when they do

38

39

40

something wrong because they don't care. They
even persuade other people to reject me, too.
They're happiest when the people around them are
as bad as they are. They choose thieves as companions, and together they take advantage of the people
and rule them harshly. Soon, they become so powerful that the people can't get out from under them.

The leaders eat well and dress well at the people's expense. They're like fat sheep who keep the
best pasture for themselves and trample the rest, or
keep the purest water for themselves and muddy the
rest. The other sheep have to eat and drink what's
been ruined by the fat sheep.

Leaders should be like good shepherds who treat
the sick among their flock, bandage the crippled,
bring back those who stray, and search everywhere
for the sheep who are lost. Bad leaders are like
shepherds who scatter and destroy the very sheep
they're supposed to be taking care of.

With leaders like these, how can people prosper?
They can't—so they end up turning on their leaders
and killing them one by one. Still, no one thinks to
ask me for help, and the people replace the leaders
they've killed with even worse ones.

Instead of turning to me, bad leaders depend on
armies for their security. Because their enemies have
to have armies to defend themselves, too, there's a
constant threat of war. Metals that could be used for
farm machinery are made into weapons; scientists
and engineers spend their time developing even
more powerful weapons to be used by soldiers
who've been trained to kill other human beings.
Even the weakest people are proud to announce that
they can carry arms.

These leaders make alliances with other rulers
in return for empty promises of assistance. Then
they double-cross the allies they're supposed to be
friends with. They talk about peace while plotting
one another's destruction; they set traps for one
another and break agreements they've made.

Nations war against each other

As long as people refuse to come back to me, the world gets worse and worse. Countries rise against countries, and nations against nations. I want you to understand how terrible war can be, so I'll describe one to you. The things I'll tell you about have actually occurred—many of them over and over again.

Picture a country that's never been invaded. Its people and their leaders feel confident that nothing bad will ever happen to them because nothing ever has. One day, an enemy marches toward them. The people hear about the enemy approaching and are terrified. Some of them run away and others try to hide like frightened animals.

The enemy soldiers descend on the country like vultures and prevent anyone else from escaping. They even pursue the people who managed to get away and drag them back. They find those who try to hide. These soldiers are known for their cruelty, and they neither pity nor spare anyone. They come from a nation that worships power and strictly disciplines its soldiers so that not one of them tires, stumbles, or sleeps during battle. They never swerve from their path or jostle one another, and nothing can stop them. They make fun of defeated leaders and their defenses as they collect captives like so many grains of sand. They're armed with the latest weapons, and are so skilled at using them that they don't miss a single target.

The enemy soldiers surround the country and swarm like flies over neighboring lands. No one can leave or enter the country because the soldiers are everywhere. The country's leaders warn the people to prepare for a siege. "Ration your food and water," they say. But the siege lasts for a long time, and the people suffer greatly. Eventually, there's such a severe shortage of food that some people even eat one another and their own children.

When the people of the country are too weak to resist, the enemy commander orders his troops to attack. The battle goes on for many days and nights without stopping; soon, only a tenth of the country's soldiers are still alive, and they start fighting among themselves. Everyone is so terrified and confused that brothers attack brothers, and neighbors attack neighbors.

The weapons and fortresses that the people were once proud of are destroyed, and the enemy soldiers flood the country like water rushing through a broken dam. The people don't realize that they are at the mercy of the soldiers—who are strangers, who speak a different language and want to kill them.

Before the war, the country had as many leaders as stars in the skies, but now nobody knows where they are. The leaders are afraid, and many try to sneak away during the night, taking only what they can carry with them. They cover their faces so no one will recognize them, but they're easily captured. The country's leaders, who once thought of themselves as gods, are completely stripped of their power. While other nations build magnificent tombs for their heads of state when they die, these leaders are killed and their bodies are thrown out without ceremony. They and their families are dumped into open and unmarked graves along with everyone else, and eventually no one even remembers their names

Business people who spent their whole lives getting and spending are forced to sell everything they have left at a loss. Soon, the country's money is worthless. Enemy soldiers are everywhere. The people lock their doors in an attempt to hide from them, but the soldiers force their way in. They rape women, and murder children in front of their parents. Wealth and status no longer matter; no one is spared.

The whole country is in turmoil. The bodies of

What hell on earth would be like (99)

those the soldiers have murdered lie in the streets. The people are frantic and confused, and trample one another in an attempt to get out of the country. Even the bravest drop everything and run for their lives. Parents desert their children, children their parents—no one gives a second thought to anything but his or her own safety. 68

69

A few people foolishly go back into their homes and gather together as many possessions as they can carry, but the soldiers are waiting for them when they try to leave. It's as if those who run away fall into a pit, and those who manage to climb out of the pit are immediately caught in a trap. Even the swiftest runners can't run fast enough; the best drivers can't drive fast enough; the strongest people aren't strong enough to force their way out. Nothing they do can help them escape; everyone is captured and there's no one to rescue them. It's as if the enemy soldiers are spreading a net over the country and gathering people in like birds. Not even the sick are allowed to go free. 70

71

72

73

Then the soldiers go through their prisoners' belongings, taking what they want and destroying everything else. They move into the people's houses, sleep in their beds, and wear their clothes. They divide the land and set boundaries wherever they please. 74, 75, 76, 77

The soldiers force many men, women, and children to leave their country and then sell them as slaves in foreign lands. The people in exile are unhappy and long for their own country the rest of their lives, but few of them ever see it again. 78, 79, 80

Other nations hear that the country has been conquered, and they themselves become frightened. "How could God let this happen?" they wonder. They don't stop to realize that it's not my fault. Terrible things like this occur when people refuse to live according to my guidelines. 81

82

Soon, it's as if the country never even existed.

Its leaders are dead and its people are scattered. It no longer has any influence in the world.

Powerful nations rise and fall

Strong nations trample weaker nations and eventually become weak themselves. Other countries war against them at the first opportunity; their power gradually disappears, too, and then they're taken over by still others. Because of this continuing process of conquering and being conquered, of warring and being warred against, the peoples of the world are ruled by many different nations, one after another. They're freed from one set of oppressive leaders only to be crushed by their so-called deliverers.

Great leaders rise and fall. They're like plants that scarcely have time to take root in the earth before the wind blows them away. Most of them are soon forgotten.

Those who are currently in power brag about themselves. "Every country in the world listens to us and fears us," they say. "No one dares to lift a finger against us." They're so proud that they start thinking of themselves as gods. Can an axe chop wood unless a person picks it up and uses it? Can a cane walk by itself? Of course not—and neither can people become as powerful as I am, regardless of how mighty they seem to be.

Strong nations fall when they choose to ignore me and my guidelines. They're so full of their own importance that they decay from within and end up destroying themselves. They betray others, and are betrayed in return. They bully others, and others bully them.

A powerful nation that's always trying to conquer other countries is like a great sea monster that believes it owns the seas and can do anything it

What hell on earth would be like

wants. One day, someone puts a hook in its jaws and hauls it out of the water. Or it's like a cedar tree that grows taller than all the other trees in the forest and thinks it's better than they are. One day, someone comes along and cuts it down.

A powerful nation's allies are always surprised and horrified when the nation falls, and they worry that they're next in line. People who were conquered by the powerful nation in the past, however, are relieved to hear about its defeat. They're glad that its leaders can no longer oppress them.

The world is full of death and destruction

The most promising young men and women all over the world are killed in the fighting among nations. So many are dead after some battles that the bodies are piled together and dumped into common graves. People become numb to the destruction around them, and don't even bother to mourn for the dead or comfort the families of those who are killed.

Women are widowed, and children are orphaned. So few men are left alive that the women fight over them. The women reach the point where they'll marry anybody and let their husbands rule over them for fear of being left alone and childless.

Cities and towns are set on fire; forests and fields are burned. Nothing can stand in the way of the flames. It's as if the ground is made of live coals and the water itself is burning; smoke and fire rise to the sky day and night. Granaries, vineyards, and farms are destroyed. Finally, there's little food left, and the happiness of harvesttime is a thing of the past.

The cities are heaps of ruins—even a little child can count the number of buildings still standing. When some people attempt to repair the ruins, others come to tear them down again. Harbors and

99 seaports that were once crowded and busy are empty
and silent. The highways are unusable and the coun-
100, tryside is deserted. Animals overrun places where
101, people once lived; at night, the air is filled with their
102 howls.

People scatter over the earth like homeless
birds. They try to escape the death and destruction
of their own countries by pleading with the leaders of
foreign nations to take them in. "Help us or we'll be
103 killed!" they beg. "Don't turn us away!"

The earth itself becomes an enemy

I promised long ago that the cycles of planting
time and harvesttime, cold and heat, summer and
winter, day and night would never end. When people are busy fighting with one another, however,
they don't work together to cope with the irregulari-
ties of nature and take good care of the earth. In a
world that's become a hell on earth, it seems as if
104 even nature is turning upside down.

Rain and hail pour down from the heavens.
While one city is flooded, another suffers from
drought. The fields wither, rivers dry up, and seas
evaporate. Vegetation along the riverbanks blows
105 away. Birds, animals, and fish perish for lack of
water. What little water remains is polluted and gradually disappears, and the earth becomes as hard as
106 iron.

People sweat and struggle in vain to make a
107 living from the land. Even though farmers plant
good seed, their crops are choked by thorns and
eaten by insects. Gardeners tend their vineyards and
fruit trees, but worms strip the bark off the vines and
108 branches before anything has a chance to ripen.

It's as if the earth wears out. Soil turns to dust
and blows away like powder, leaving bare rocks on

What hell on earth would be like

which nothing can grow. The land becomes good for nothing.

Famine spreads everywhere, and people are forced to ration what little food they have. Birds and animals are so hungry that they become sickly and desert the few offspring they bear. They attack human beings and turn on the same people who used to care for them.

The sky is filled with strange disturbances. Whirlwinds blow and storms rage uncontrollably. Clouds of smoke blacken the sky, which looks as if it's in mourning for the terrible times. Day after day, darkness and gloom cover the land. The clouds are so thick that the sun's rays can't penetrate them; it wouldn't make any difference if the sun never rose at all.

The seas churn violently, and waves pound on the shores. Whole countries are destroyed by floods, and islands disappear beneath tidal waves. Volcanoes erupt, pouring lava into the valleys; earthquakes move mountains back and forth; rocks crack and crumble into dust. People have treated the earth so badly that it seems to be writhing in pain.

People get desperate

Disaster follows disaster; rumor follows rumor. Societies crumble and fall apart. There are no more judges, lawyers, doctors, scholars, artists, or business people left.

People get desperate for someone to lead them. A man grabs his brother by the arm, saying, "You lead us out of this mess."

"I can barely keep myself alive!" his brother answers. "How can I possibly help anyone else? Leave me alone!"

The clergy are powerless; those who are left

spend their time mourning because the houses of worship have been ruined. False prophets have desecrated them, robbers have stripped them, and armies 119 have damaged them until only the shells remain.

The old order is replaced by a new one. People who were once important are removed from power. Others who know nothing about leadership are put 120 in charge.

Wealthy people who used to brag about their riches as they lay around on expensive couches find that their money is worthless, and they're as poor as 121 everyone else. When they were rich they watched to see whether people were admiring them as they passed by; now they're hungry and dressed in rags, and they cover their faces because they're ashamed 122 of what's happened to them.

Soon, people everywhere live in makeshift shelters and eat whatever they can find. Disease spreads so quickly that when one person in a family gets sick, everyone else does, too. People cry out against me 123 and their leaders. They don't laugh because there's nothing left to be happy about; their songs are filled 124 with despair. Even men and women who never cried before in their lives now weep bitterly because of what they've lost. "We're ruined!" they wail. "Look at 125 what's become of us!"

Every day, messengers bring reports of more and more disasters. People get so frightened that they tremble all the time. They put their fingers in their ears and squeeze their eyes shut so they won't 126 hear or see any more of the trouble around them.

"You're lucky you never had children!" parents say to those who are childless. They can hardly take care of themselves, much less look after their children.

Living has become so difficult that people want to die. "Fall on us," they beg the mountains. "Cover 127 us," they plead with the hills. Those who do manage to survive get weaker every day. Eventually, many go crazy because of all the misery around them. No one even remembers the people who've died along the way; it's as if they never existed at all.

The world ends

The hell on earth I've been describing is terrible for everyone. Even the people who faithfully keep my agreement suffer because of what's happening around them. I look after them, however, and protect them at all times; I know if a single hair on one person's head is harmed. Like a gardener who refuses to throw away a cluster of grapes if only a few of them are good, I won't permit the world to be completely destroyed as long as some people still live according to my guidelines.

If there's even one person who doesn't know about me, I make sure that some of my followers survive. When everyone has had a chance to hear about me, however, and has rejected me, I remove the last of my servants from the hell on earth. By this time, there's no goodness left anywhere, and people kill each other off. Animals, fish, and birds die, too. No one escapes; no one is left alive. This is how the world ends.

Can you see how terrible a hell on earth would be? This isn't what I want for you! All of the trouble I've described to you can be avoided if you and others choose to live according to the guidelines I've set up. I've offered to make an agreement with you because I want you to live the good life and do your part to change the world into a heaven on earth instead of a hell on earth. I'll explain what the good life is like—and then I'll tell you how the world can become a heaven on earth.

IX
WHAT THE GOOD LIFE IS LIKE

I give you a new heart and my spirit

I've explained what happens to you when you choose not to live according to my guidelines. Your thinking becomes twisted, and soon you no longer care for yourself, for me, or for anyone else. You not only hurt yourself, but you're also a bad influence in the world. If you don't come back to me, you end up destroying yourself.

If, on the other hand, you choose to keep my agreement, you become an entirely different person. It's as if I take your old heart out and give you a new one. You no longer want to do anything to harm your relationship with me. You know me well, love me completely, and wouldn't turn away from me for the world. You love the people around you as much as you love yourself, and you love yourself because you know that I love you.

I fill you with my spirit. You can compare my spirit to the wind; even though you can't see the

(106)

What the good life is like· (107)

wind, you can see what it does. My spirit is invisible like the wind, but its effects are obvious both within you and around you. My spirit is like a little voice inside of you that tells you when you're doing something wrong. It reminds you that you're being good to yourself when you live according to my guidelines.

People who choose not to follow me don't know what my spirit is like and can't experience it. They aren't guided or helped by it—they don't even recognize it. You're different, though, because you keep my agreement. My spirit lives in you and is always with you; you know it when you hear it, and welcome its advice.

My spirit comforts you, helps you to distinguish right from wrong, reminds you of my words, and prepares you for the future. It guides you to what's best for you all your life. If you start to wander off the path, my spirit whispers in your ear, "Don't do that. Here's the way to go."

You no longer stumble around in confusion; you know where you're coming from and where you're going. You realize that the path my spirit is leading you down is straight rather than crooked, level rather than rough, and you can walk with confidence. Just as the sun chases away the darkness at dawn, my spirit floods your way with light. Your life is so full of light that it seems as if the moon is as bright as the sun, and the sun is as bright as it would be if seven days' worth of sunlight were shining down all at once.

You get wiser and more understanding all the time. You know the truth when you see it; you can tell what's good from what's bad. You can easily identify those who follow me and those who don't. As long as you keep my agreement, my spirit stays with you, guiding and counseling you for the rest of your life.

You and I have a special relationship

When you choose to follow me and listen to what my spirit tells you, you're precious to me. You and I have a very special relationship. It's as if we're married and living together in the same home. We belong to each other forever. Even though you're my servant in the world, I don't treat you like a servant; instead, I see you as a close friend and confidant.

You're my own darling child. I give you my name, and I write it down next to the names of all the other people who live according to my guidelines. We're a family. I comfort you as a mother comforts her child. I treat you with compassion and kindness. Even if the mountains and hills disappeared, and everything in the world changed completely, I'd keep on loving you and would love you forever.

Because you're special to me, I want you to know all about me. So I open your ears and teach you to recognize my voice. Morning after morning, I awaken you and talk to you. I share secrets with you—hidden and wonderful things about me and the world. Although I realize that you aren't able to grasp everything I'm saying all at once, I know that someday you'll understand what I'm talking about.

The more time you spend listening to me, the more you come to realize who I am—the living God. It becomes clear to you that there's no one else like me anywhere. Eventually, you know so much about me that you can accurately describe me to others. This is one reason I teach you about myself—so that you'll turn around and spread the truth about me.

The only people who can ever really know me are those I speak to personally; or those who hear about me from others who know me. I don't reveal myself to just anybody; people who refuse to keep my agreement can never know me. They may look high and low, but they won't see me; they may listen as hard as they can, but they won't hear me. It's as if I talk to them in a language they can't understand.

On the other hand, because things are right between you and me, I speak personally to you and reveal myself to you. You understand more and more of what I'm saying. It's something like this: Those who already have some knowledge of me are given even more, while those who don't have any real knowledge of me to begin with lose even the little they think they have. 17

I answer your prayers

I always hear you when you pray to me. Whenever you call me, I answer, "Here I am!" Because I know what you need even before you ask me for it, I sometimes answer your prayers ahead of time. 18

I do whatever you ask me to do if it's in your best interests. Don't give up, however, if I seem slow in answering your prayers. For example, if you went to a friend's house at midnight and said, "Please lend me a loaf of bread—I don't have any food and unexpected company has just arrived," your friend might answer without even opening the door, "Don't bother me—I'm in bed!" But if you kept pleading with your friend, he or she would finally get up and give you a loaf of bread. In the same way, keep asking me for what you need and I'll eventually give it to you if it's good for you. 19

I'll tell you a story to help you understand this.

There was once a judge who didn't care about anyone or anything but himself. A poor widow kept coming to him and begging, "Please help me! My creditors are after me, and I don't have anywhere else to turn!"

The judge wouldn't even listen to her at first, but when she refused to give up he finally said to himself, "It's clear that this widow is going to keep pestering me, so I may as well do what she wants."

The judge gave in and helped the widow—and he didn't even like her. Imagine how much more willing I am to give you what you need—all you have to do is ask! So don't quit praying just because I don't give you what you want right away. Ask, and you'll receive; seek, and you'll find; knock, and the door will be opened to you.

If your children wanted bread, would you give them a stone? If they were hungry for fish, would you hand them a snake? Of course not! Even people who don't keep my agreement try to give their children what they need. Think about how much more I'd like to give to you!

When you ask for things I want you to have, and believe strongly enough that you'll get them, you will. It's as if you could say to a mountain, "Get up and throw yourself into the sea," and it would, or you could say to a tree, "Uproot yourself and plant yourself over there," and it would do what you asked. Even if your faith in me is as small as a mustard seed, I'll answer your prayers.

I take good care of you

You never need to worry that I'll fail you or abandon you. Does a mother forget the baby she's nursing? Of course not—but even if she did, I wouldn't forget you. You're the apple of my eye; I think about you all the time. It's as if your name were written on the palm of my hand.

I watch over you night and day. Whenever you need my help, I take your hand and guide you. "Don't be afraid," I reassure you. "I'm with you." I'm like a shade tree that protects you from the heat of the day, or a shelter in a storm. I hide you in the shadow of my hand. You never have to run away from danger or flee from trouble, for I walk in front of you and guard you from behind at the same time. You're as safe with me as you would be if you were inside a strong fortress high on a cliff.

When you go through deep water, I keep you from drowning. When you walk through fire, I protect you from the flames. I carry you when you're weary, and I'm there to catch you when you stumble. Everybody falls once in a while; when you do, however, I give you the strength to get up again. It's as if you can fly with the wings of an eagle; you can run without feeling faint; you can walk without getting tired.

Good parents discipline their children to teach them how to behave. In the same way, I may let you go through troubles from time to time if that's what it takes to help you become a better person. After all, living the good life means much more than just having enough to eat and drink—it also means listening to me and taking my words to heart. Sometimes, the only way to find this out is by experiencing problems firsthand. Keep in mind, though, that I always know what's happening to you. I'm with you even when you feel lonely or are far from home, and I make sure that you never lack anything.

You can compare my relationship with you to the one a shepherd has with the sheep. I'm like a good shepherd; I know my own sheep, and they know me. My sheep come to me when they hear my voice, and would never follow a stranger. I call each of my sheep by name, and they know they're safe with me. I walk ahead of them, carrying the lambs in my arms next to my heart and gently leading those with young.

I guide my sheep along paths they're unfamiliar with to good pastures and springs of fresh water. When they've had enough to eat and drink, I encourage them to lie down and rest. If one of them gets hurt in any way, I tenderly treat its wounds until it's well again. If one of them goes astray, I look for it until I find it and bring it back to join the others.

I'm not like hired servants who run away and leave the sheep whenever a wolf comes—they don't care about the sheep because the sheep don't belong to them. I love my sheep so much that I'd willingly die for them. I take such good care of them that nothing bad could happen to them.

When I lead my sheep back to the sheepfold, the gatekeeper opens the door. The sheepfold has only one door, and only my sheep and I can go through it. I have several flocks of sheep, and not all of them belong to this particular sheepfold. I want to bring all of my sheep together someday. Then there'll be one flock under one shepherd.

I make you strong

People who reject me may spread rumors about you, stand in your way whenever they can, and try to walk all over you because you keep my agreement. They may even claim that I've told them to make things difficult for you. You may feel trapped by them, and think that you're powerless against them. Don't be afraid of them! Watch and see what I do to help you.

Imagine a vineyard so lovely that a song could be written about it. The keeper waters it carefully and guards it night and day. No one dares to come near it without the keeper's permission. You're my vineyard, and I'm your keeper. I watch over you and protect you at all times. I never neglect you even for a second. Nothing can touch you without first having to deal with me.

I'm an enemy to your enemies, and my anger toward them is like a flood that destroys everything in its path. It's like a violent storm full of wind, rain, and hailstones. A lion growling over its prey pays no

What the good life is like

attention to someone shouting at it from a distance; in the same way, I'm not afraid of your enemies, no matter how powerful they may seem to you. I drive them away from you and punish them for threatening you.

I turn their own weapons against them. They get confused and don't know what to do from one minute to the next. They no longer have the presence of mind to harm you. They're so busy with their own problems that they don't have time to worry about you.

Your enemies run away from me like dust stirred up by the wind. Even though they may frighten you in the evening, I'll make sure that they're gone when morning comes. You may think that your enemies are as strong as oak trees, but I do away with them little by little until there's nothing left of them. I crush them like straw; I gather them into piles and burn them, and then carry away the ashes.

The more closely you live according to my guidelines, the stronger you become. You stop turning pale when something or someone threatens you. You grow more and more like me every day until your enemies no longer have any influence over you at all. You're as unyielding to them as a stone wall.

My words that you speak are as powerful as a forest fire. My message is like a sword in your hands; you can use it to protect yourself from anyone who threatens you. Because of me you become so strong that nothing bad can really hurt you anymore. It's as if you could walk barefoot across poisonous snakes or scorpions and they wouldn't harm you. No one is able to stand up to you.

You learn to turn people's weapons against them, just as I've taught you to do. Your enemies may come at you from one direction, but they'll flee from you in seven. You pursue them tirelessly until they can no longer run away and they fall down in front of you. You walk over them as if they're nothing but ashes beneath your feet. Those who used to torment you now fear you. Even though you're only one against them, you're more powerful than all of them put together.

With my help, you gradually subdue all your enemies. You look high and low for more, but you can't find any. "Where are all the people who wanted to make trouble for me?" you call out. "Come and challenge me!" Because I'm at your side, though, you're so strong that no one dares to step forward. Just as a hungry man dreams of eating but wakes up hungry, or a thirsty woman dreams of drinking but wakes up thirsty, your enemies may imagine themselves conquering you—but their dreams will never come true.

I bless you

You may have spent part of your life rejecting me and doing other things to hurt yourself. When you choose to live according to my guidelines, however, I give back to you whatever you lost when you weren't following me—and much more. You prosper more than you ever thought possible.

I bless you and all the other people who keep my agreement more than I bless anyone else. When you give up something for me, you receive a hundred times more in return. It's as if I open the windows of heaven and pour down blessings on you. Like leaves overflowing the sides of a basket, my gifts to you are much more than you can hold at any one time—and this is only the beginning.

I bless you wherever you go and whatever you do. You may have heard about people who follow me and who are very successful; I delight in seeing this happen, and in seeing you prosper, too. Instead of working hard and getting nowhere, you're richly

What the good life is like (115)

rewarded for your efforts. You spend your time and energy in satisfying ways. You seem to be growing taller and taller all the time. You're able to influence others without having to compromise yourself. People see you as an example of how well I treat my followers.

56

57

You never have to worry about your family name dying out; your descendants are as numerous as sand in the sea or stars in the sky. If they follow me, too, they thrive like grass by water or willows by flowing streams.

58

You're happy

Even if you eat all the food you want, you get hungry again; even if you drink all the water you want, you get thirsty again. When you keep my agreement, though, you have all the spiritual food and drink you'll ever need and you feel satisfied. I give you the kind of peace that you can't find anywhere else. You're one with me and the world, and at rest within yourself.

59

60

When you do something wrong and hurt yourself, I heal your wounds. You don't suffer from any of the terrible diseases that occur because people are unhappy or don't take good care of themselves. You grow like a garden that I myself water and watch over. You blossom like a lily; you're as lovely as an olive tree or a cool spring whose waters never run out. You're like a noble cedar full of leafy branches that fears neither heat nor drought.

61

62

63,
64, 65

I give you joy that lasts forever. You laugh and sing; you're as happy as a calf let out to pasture. Your children rejoice with you. Just as the earth brings forth green shoots and a garden fills with fruits and vegetables, you can't help praising me for all the wonderful things I do for you. You thank me every day for making you as prosperous as you are.

66

67

After a child is born, the mother forgets all about her labor pains because she's overjoyed about her new baby. You, too, forget how unhappy you were before you turned to me. I don't remember the trouble you had in the past, and neither do you.

You're good for the world

I made you to be like me and do my work in the world. Don't worry if you aren't as attractive as you'd like to be, or if you don't come from an important family. When you keep my agreement, I give you whatever you need to be my servant. Imagine people out in a boat trying to catch fish. You're like them, except that you're bringing other people to me rather than catching fish.

I'm the one who sends you into the world, so whoever accepts you accepts me, and whoever turns you away turns me away, too. I'm happy when people welcome you with open arms. Even if they give you as little as a cup of cold water when you're thirsty, I reward them for being good to you.

Don't ever be afraid that you won't know what to say when the time comes for you to speak up about me. If I want you to talk for me, I'll open your mouth and give you all the right words. If I don't want you to speak, you'll feel as if your tongue is stuck to the roof of your mouth and you won't be able to say a thing. Your words from me will be so wise and good that no one will be able to win an argument against you. You'll be able to prove your point whenever anyone tries to contradict you or make a fool of you.

If you tell people that I'll do something, I'll do it because I stand behind everything you say. Your listeners will learn that you speak the truth and that you're talking for me. I'll go along with any agreement you make with someone else or any contract

What the good life is like

you dissolve with someone else. Whenever you and even one or two others gather in my name, I'll be right there with you.

When people make amends for what they've done wrong and choose to live according to my guidelines, you may tell them that I forgive them. You may find that they react to what you say in many different ways. For example, some may appear to be less grateful than others. If this happens, don't let it worry you. A man once loaned money to two other men; he gave a great deal to one and a smaller amount to the other. When they couldn't pay him back, he canceled both their loans. Which of the two men do you suppose loved him the most after that? The one who had owed him the most! You, too, may find that people who are forgiven for many things treat you better than those who are forgiven for a few.

Once in a while, it may seem as if nothing you say or do has any affect whatsoever. You may feel you're wasting your breath on people who couldn't care less about what you're trying to tell them. Don't give up! Everything you do in my name accomplishes something, no matter how futile it seems at the time.

Wherever you go, it's as if the blind can see again, the lame can walk, and the deaf can hear. Those who seemed to be spiritually dead come to life again, and the sick recover. On the other hand, people who think that they don't need your help or mine show how foolish they really are—they're blind and don't know it.

You're amazed when you see all the wonderful things you can do because of me, and I help you to do even greater works than these. You become like me and act as I would act, and because you're so close to me I let you know everything I'm doing.

You're good for the world. You bring parents and children back together again; you reunite people who've been lost to each other and teach them how to love again. You're as refreshing as dew on the grass or a cool rain that's long overdue. You're like someone who opens a prison door and lets everyone inside go free. Just as the sun rises at dawn to chase the darkness away, you bring light and happiness into the world.

You're bad for the people who reject you, though. They hate you and try to stop you, but nothing they do can affect you. They're as helpless against you as if they were a flock of sheep and you were a lion in their midst.

You're like a rock; people can depend on you and take you at your word. You and others like you form the foundations of the heaven on earth I want the world to be. Nothing can ever shake you or stand in your way.

You live forever

Long ago, when I first made the world, I said that people would only live on the earth for short periods of time. They're made of dust, and they return to dust. If you follow me all your days, however, you'll live to a ripe old age. And, when your time on the earth is at an end, you won't just cease to exist; even though your body will die, you'll live forever.

In the Bible you can read these words, "I'm the God of Abraham, the God of Isaac, and the God of Jacob." Those men died long before these words were written, yet I speak of them as if they were still alive—because they are. The moon fades away, but it always reappears in the sky three days later. In the same way, you die and I raise you up again, just as I raised up Abraham, Isaac, and Jacob.

I come for you and take you to live with me. My house has many rooms, and I've prepared some of them especially for you. I wouldn't tell you this if it weren't true. Your life with me is far better than anything you could ever imagine. You never again have to worry about day-to-day problems. You stay with me forever.

I've been telling you what'll happen to you if you keep my agreement because I want you to understand how wonderful the good life is. If you live according to the guidelines I've set up, you not only benefit yourself, but you're also a good influence in the world. If everyone decided to follow me, the world would become a heaven on earth. I'll explain what I mean by this.

X
WHAT HEAVEN ON EARTH WOULD BE LIKE

People praise my followers

When you carefully live according to my guidelines, you're a different person than you would be if you didn't. You love me, you love other people, and you're at peace with yourself. You live the good life. If more and more people keep my agreement, they can eventually change the world into a heaven on earth—a wonderful place full of goodness and joy. This is what I intended the world to be when I made it.

Of course, this sort of thing won't happen overnight—it takes time. Even when it seems hopeless, though—when no one listens to you, or when people harass you for following me—I don't want you to get discouraged. I'll describe how the world can become a heaven on earth because I want you to recognize the signs and do your part to help this take place.

Heaven on earth can begin even if only a handful of people carefully live according to my guide-

What heaven on earth would be like (121)

lines no matter what. If they tell others about me, and these people turn around and tell their friends, too, love and peace spread everywhere. People who accept and encourage my followers instead of criticizing them also help to make the world a better place.

When my servants are no longer penalized for following me, some of them rise to positions of importance. People notice them and say, "Those who do what God wants seem to be wiser and more understanding than those who don't. God answers their prayers, and they lead happy, productive lives. They're good to have around." More and more people begin to realize who I am—the living God—and to see that I bless anyone who keeps my agreement. This makes them stop and think. "It must be worthwhile to live according to God's guidelines after all," they say to themselves.

People who used to persecute my servants start to regret it, and do their best to make up for the unkind things they said and did in the past. They discourage anyone who wants to make trouble for my followers. As a result, those who love me are free to talk about me, and become well known in the world. Powerful leaders seek them out and do nice things for them.

This change in attitude is remarkable. My servants were once like stones that workers rejected, but now they are like cornerstones chosen for important buildings. People respect them and turn to them for advice and guidance. The world is on its way to becoming a heaven on earth.

People turn to me

People everywhere start to realize that false gods can't make them happy. They turn from the things they used to consider important and seek me out instead. When they discover that the only way to live the good life is by following me, many of them decide to give up their old habits and keep my agreement. They try to persuade others, too. "Stop doing things that only hurt you," they say. "Do what God wants, and you'll be much better off."

My servants make it easy for others to come back to me. They point out that it's really simpler in the long run to live according to my guidelines. It's as if they go ahead of everyone else and build a straight road that people can travel on to me; the road has no obstacles or detours, and no one has any questions about which way to go.

The message my followers bring is like the call of a trumpet; people from one end of the earth to the other can hear it. Not everyone takes it seriously, though. Sometimes people who seem exactly alike in every other way will respond differently to the call. For example, two farmers working together in a field will hear it, and one will gladly answer while the other won't. Two cooks will be preparing food side by side, and one will say, "Yes, God," while the other won't. But no matter where people are or what they're doing, they'll all hear the trumpet call. How they choose to respond is up to each person individually.

People from all walks of life come to me. Some are in trouble; some aren't. Some feel trapped by their own thinking; others are blind, crippled, or sick. I welcome each and every one of them with open arms. Like a shepherd who brings the sheep to the sheepfold, I gather in all who want to keep my agreement. I forgive and heal them.

Many people who openly rejected me in the past have second thoughts. They realize that they're suffering because of the bad things they've done. They want to change, but they don't know how. "What can we do to straighten out our lives?" they ask one

What heaven on earth would be like (123)

another. "God's followers will know. Let's find out from them." They travel great distances to seek my servants' help. They bring offerings for me and gifts for them, and shyly ask about me.

Important leaders who used to make trouble for my followers now sit at their feet like children and want to hear about my agreement. People who speak other languages go in search of my servants. "We've heard that God is with you," they say. "Please tell us everything you know about God."

None of these people, regardless of what their pasts may have been, need to worry that they'll be rejected or scorned. Even though they may have threatened my followers at one time or done them harm, they're all treated with love. My servants willingly teach them my guidelines so that they, too, can live the good life.

People who turn away from me are like bones in a graveyard. Once they choose to follow me, though, it's as if I go into the graveyard, open the graves, and take out the bones. Then I put flesh on them and breathe life into them. The dead bones become living human beings who get up and walk away into a new life. People who refuse to come back to me, however, never know what it's like to come alive again. They spend their days fooling themselves. They don't realize that they're just as dead as the bones in a grave.

The people who choose to come to me dedicate their talents and possessions to me and my work in the world. They do their best to change the world into a heaven on earth. It isn't always easy, though. In spite of their efforts, not everyone turns to me, and not everyone who does continues to keep my agreement. Some people are so full of hatred that they try to stop those who work for me. My servants have to deal with them before the world can become a better place.

Troublemakers are stopped

The people who absolutely refuse to keep my agreement carry on with business as usual. They eat, drink, marry one another, buy, sell, plant, and build, but they don't bother to straighten things out with me or each other. Because they don't want me in their lives, they're amazed when so many other people choose to live according to my guidelines.

My servants start to realize that they can't accomplish as much by working alone as they could if they worked together. It becomes obvious to them that arguing among themselves is a waste of time and energy, so they get organized and make plans to fight together against the bad things in the world. They attract as much attention as lightning that flashes across the sky and illuminates it from one end to the other. Soon they have more power and influence than they ever had before.

The people who want to stop my work in the world get uneasy when they see how strong my followers are becoming, so they turn around and get organized, too. They cause as much trouble as they can, hoping to frighten and confuse my servants. They want to scatter them once and for all.

If you notice these things happening around you, don't be afraid. When a tree starts sprouting new leaves, you know that summer is near; in the same way, you can tell that a better world is close at hand when my servants start working together and people who hate them feel threatened by them.

The troublemakers arm themselves with the most sophisticated weapons, and seem to be everywhere at once, like a storm cloud that covers the land. They think that my servants are vulnerable and can easily be overpowered—but they're mistaken. They don't stop to realize that I look out for those who keep my agreement and work against those who don't.

What heaven on earth would be like

The people who want to harm my followers become unhappy, confused, and sick, and begin to fight among themselves. The earth quakes, mountains fall, and rocks split in two; rain and hailstones pour down from the skies. These hateful people are terrified; they run away and try to hide. Instead of scattering my servants, they themselves are scattered. 29

In the meantime, my followers get stronger and stronger all the time. Each of them is like a heavy stone; whoever tries to move it gets hurt. The people 30 who hate them see how little power they really have and lose all their confidence. 31

Many of the troublemakers end up being killed or put away. You may think that this is harsh or unfair. As long as they insist on making things difficult for my servants, however, and doing what they can to prevent the world from becoming a heaven on earth, they have to be stopped. 32

My followers are happy when they realize that no one will ever make trouble for them again. I call 33 them to me and tenderly say, "Your problems are almost over. Soon, you'll have peace for all time." 34

Bad things have to go

Even when the troublemakers are no longer a threat, there's still work left to do. Shepherds put 35 goats in one pen and sheep in another, and farmers winnow chaff from wheat. In the same way, any people who still refuse to keep my agreement have to be separated from those who follow it. 36

This story will help you to understand what I mean.

There was once a man who planted wheat in his field. One night, while his employees were asleep, some of his enemies came and sowed weeds in the field. Soon, both weeds and wheat were growing up side by side. The man's employees were puzzled. "Where did all these weeds come from?" they asked him.

"From my enemies," he answered.

"Should we go out and pull them up?" they wanted to know.

"No," he said. "If you pull up the weeds, you may accidentally uproot the wheat, too. Let them both grow up together until harvesttime. Then separate the weeds from the wheat. Tie the weeds into bundles and burn them, but put the wheat into my barn."

I'm like the man who planted wheat; the field is like the world, the wheat like my servants, and the weeds like the people who refuse to live according to my guidelines. I allow bad and good to exist side by side, just as the man in the story did, until it's time to
37 separate them from each other.

"You're going to live in a wonderful world," I say to the people who've been keeping my agreement.
38 Those who've rejected me get a second chance; if it's clear that they'll never live according to my guidelines, though, they have to go. They can't be part of
39 heaven on earth.

For example, hypocrites can't stay. Some of them tell me, "God, we did everything you wanted us to do, we talked about you all the time, and we prayed to you every day. Don't be so hard on us! You remember us, don't you?"

"I don't know you at all," I answer.

Hypocrites are like people who went to a prince's wedding without being properly dressed. The king walked up to them and asked, "How on earth did you get in here, dressed like that?" They didn't know what to say, so the king told his servants, "Throw these fools out. They'll ruin the celebration if they stay." Just as the king didn't want these people at his son's wedding, I don't allow hypocrites in
40 heaven on earth. They'd spoil it for the rest.

What heaven on earth would be like

People who like to walk all over others and people who think they're better than everyone else can't stay. Neither can those who refuse to take good care of themselves; they spread disease, eat bad food, and live in unsanitary surroundings.

In the same way, people who still insist on worshiping false gods—anything or anyone other than me—aren't permitted in the new world. When these people find out that what they put their trust in can't do anything for them, they're terrified.

"Somebody help us!" they plead.

"Ask your gods to help you," I say.

Other people who used to serve false gods are ashamed of themselves, like thieves who are embarrassed when they're caught in the act. They forget all about other gods and never think about them again.

False prophets—who especially irritate me—aren't allowed to stay, either. They claim that they speak for me, but they don't. They say that they want to help people, but they can't. Because they're confused themselves, no one who listens to them ever finds out how to live the good life.

The sayings of false prophets are like a coat of whitewash on a mud house. The first time it rains, the walls crumble and the people inside are drenched. "Why didn't you tell us that the house was made of mud?" they ask the person who sold it to them. "You whitewashed it so it would look better than it really was! You tricked us!" The salesperson certainly didn't do them any favors; in the same way, false prophets don't do any good for those who pay attention to them.

All the false prophets in the world are exposed as the fools they really are. They couldn't solve problems for anyone else, and now they can't figure out how to help themselves. They don't even have enough sense to come back to me, so they can't stay in the heaven on earth.

Finally, my servants and I deal with sorcerers,

mediums, and others like them—they're fools, just as false prophets are. The things they see aren't really there at all; their words are nonsense; the comfort they give is empty. Some of them sell clothing and jewelry that supposedly have magical powers. For a few pennies, they tell lies that turn people away from me. They discourage those who try to follow me and encourage those who don't. My servants spread the word that so-called magical clothes and jewelry don't have any powers, and those who bought them throw them away. People quit following anyone but me.

The people on earth are no longer misled by false prophets, sorcerers, and the like, so they quit being superstitious and refuse to take part in any more meaningless rituals. Instead of acting out of fear and ignorance, they know the truth and follow it. By this time, everyone has made things right with me; everyone is living according to my guidelines.

People do what's good

I've said that the world could be a heaven on earth if everyone carefully kept my agreement. When all the people who refused to live according to my guidelines are gone, and everything else bad or harmful has been done away with, I keep my promise. Does a woman go through labor and delivery without having a baby? Of course not! Neither do I bring the new world to the brink of being born without following through.

The new world isn't a bit like the old one. Soon, people don't even think about the way things used to be because they're so delighted with the way things are. They realize that I'm one God and the only God. Everyone calls me by the same name. No one turns away from me anymore.

My influence can be felt everywhere. People of all nations and faiths have chosen to follow me, so they don't fight among themselves as they used to, but instead work together for the good of all. I live in this heaven on earth and people welcome me. They're happy to do what I ask them to; they recognize how good and loving I am, and realize that I have their best interests at heart. Each person overflows with my spirit. Children talk about me with their parents, and parents with their children. Old and young alike dream of the things they can accomplish with my help.

People everywhere are willing to listen to me, and I teach them all about myself. I no longer need messengers to spread my news because everyone knows me. Men, women, and children live according to my guidelines. Instead of being confused, they learn how to behave wisely. Someone who used to do things on impulse now shows good judgment in all kinds of situations. Anyone who once had trouble talking can now speak easily and distinctly. The blind and deaf can see and hear.

The whole world has been turned around. In the past, many people reached positions of power by tricking others or walking all over them. Now, those who try hardest to keep my agreement are the ones who hold the highest positions and are the most popular. While people used to be admired for rejecting me or getting away with things, now someone who's lax in living according to my guidelines isn't even given the time of day.

Everyone treats everyone else politely and considerately, and tries to be the best person that he or she can be. People are rewarded for being kind and loving. Arguments are settled quickly and easily. The legal system functions smoothly; decisions handed down by judges and juries are reasonable and well thought out. No one has to worry that he or she won't get a fair trial, because people tell the truth. There are no more false witnesses or judges who can be bribed.

People choose wise men and women to be their

leaders. These leaders aren't strangers to the people, and they don't oppress them. They're kind, fair, and quick to apologize when they do something wrong. They don't use their powers to gain unfair advantage over others; instead, they do their best to help those who are weaker than they are. They care for others just as a mother tenderly protects her child during a storm. Religious leaders are careful to listen to me and avoid misleading anyone. They work peacefully with political leaders.

The people love both their political and religious leaders and are eager to support and follow them. They see these leaders as godlike and loving. The leaders govern justly and kindly, and the people are willing to do whatever they ask. Everyone prospers.

The world is peaceful

Because no one fights with anyone else, people live and work together in harmony. They're never forced from their homes, as they were in the old world; no one is ever again evicted, banished, or exiled. It's as if each person is planted firmly in the ground and can't be uprooted.

Rather than quarreling over who's right or wrong about a matter, people who follow different religions, come from different cultures, or hold different political views cooperate with one another. Violence and destruction are things of the past. No one oppresses or terrorizes anyone else. Women don't have to be protected by men, and children can safely play wherever they wish.

People quit learning how to war against each other. Since no one in the new world needs military strength or protection, there are no more armies marching back and forth or navies patrolling the seas. Instead of spending time, money, and materials

What heaven on earth would be like

on weapons, people use their energy to produce enough food for everyone.

Even animals are affected by the peaceful atmosphere in the world. They never again attack people out of fear or hunger, and anyone who wants to can sleep soundly in a dark woods or travel safely through a wilderness.

The wolf and the lamb live together and share the same food, and the leopard sleeps beside the young goat. The lion and the cow exist side by side, and their young frolic with each other in the fields. Children can play near snakes and handle them without danger. In the new world, no one hurts anyone else.

Things that used to frighten or injure people aren't around any longer. There are no harmful plants or animals or stinging insects; bushes don't even have thorns. The world is at rest, and people feel secure. They trust one another, and don't hesitate to ask strangers into their homes. They don't need to lock their doors or put up fences to keep intruders out because they aren't afraid anymore. The new world is as stable as a tent with stakes that can't be pulled up or cords that can't be broken. Nothing is allowed to disturb the harmony of this heaven on earth.

The earth is fruitful again

Everyone works together to take good care of the earth. People learn how to use its resources wisely and carefully and make up for the harm that was done to it in the past. If they take something from the earth, they do their best to replace it and maintain the balance of nature. I heal the earth's wounds, and restore it to the way I first intended it to be. Soon, no part of it is useless or barren.

People are prepared for rain regardless of when

it falls, and know how to use it to their best advantage. Lush vegetation springs up everywhere, and crops are cultivated and harvested all year long.
69 Creeks that were once dry are now full of fresh water; clear streams flow through the wilderness, and springs are discovered in the desert. People learn how to use them to irrigate new fields and forests. Flowers bloom in places where only thorns grew
70 before.

Polluted waters become clean again and swarm with all sorts of living things. Anyone can safely swim in them and drink from them. Trees thrive along the
71 riverbanks. People learn to use the seas for the good of all, and harvest the fish and plants that grow there. Precautions are taken so floods won't occur, even
72 when waves toss and roar during storms.

Strong winds, too much or too little sun, and
73 heat or cold out of season no longer bother anyone. People have learned how to cope with the irregulari-
74 ties of nature, and are ready for whatever happens.

Everyone is amply rewarded for the work he or she does. Insects, worms, and diseases don't threaten or destroy what has been planted as they did in the
75, past, and there's always a surplus of healthy crops at
76, harvesttime. Because the world bears so much food,
77 no one ever goes hungry again. Even wild animals have enough to eat.

The earth has become a delightful place that seems to flow with milk and honey; it's as if the mountains themselves drip with wine. Rivers of clean water flow among the hills and through the valleys. Wheat, barley, grapes, fig trees, pomegranates, and olives are plentiful. I personally take care of this heaven on earth, and I watch over it year after
78 year to make sure that no one ever lacks anything.

It's as if I've spread a wonderful feast for all my followers. They eat their fill of plump fruits, crisp vegetables, and choice meats, and quench their thirst with fine wine. People all over the world enjoy
79 the things I've given them.

What heaven on earth would be like

Everyone is happy and prosperous

I give back whatever people lost when the world wasn't a heaven on earth—and more. Men, women, and children thrive and have everything they need. Nobody's poor or disadvantaged anymore. 80

New cities spring up everywhere, and damaged buildings are repaired. People can put up their own homes wherever they please and live in them as long as they like. Cities are rebuilt with precious metals 81 and stones. Instead of bronze, they're made of gold; instead of iron, they're made of silver. The new world is more beautiful than the old one ever was. 82

The heaven on earth that my servants and I have made is like a mother who tenderly cares for her children; she nurses them, carries them on her hips, and lovingly holds them in her lap. Her children are satisfied because all their needs are met. In the same way, everyone is taken care of in the new world. 83

People are so happy that they sing and dance, and play joyfully on musical instruments. There's no reason to commemorate sad occasions anymore because none occur. Even the elderly dance merrily in the streets. Each person's face shines like a crown set with jewels. Despair and misery are things of the past. Nature rejoices, too. The mountains and hills sing, and the trees clap their hands. Everything in the new world is filled with joy. 84

People from one end of the earth to the other praise me. "Thank you for being so good to us, God!" they say. "We know now how much you love us." I'm delighted to see how happy and prosperous 85 everyone is; I'm as excited as a bride and groom on their wedding day. 86

Everywhere in the new world, people take good care of themselves. They learn how to prevent diseases and keep their bodies strong and healthy. Women who want to have children are able to do so, 87 since miscarriages and other difficulties during pregnancy no longer occur. Parents don't have to worry that their children will die young. Everyone lives a long life.

The world fills with loving, happy people. Old men and women sit on their doorsteps watching boys and girls play together. Families continue from generation to generation, with many descendants to carry on their family names.

How long does this heaven on earth last? As long as people continue to keep my agreement. Just as I wouldn't alter the laws of nature, I wouldn't change my mind about blessing those who live according to my guidelines. I am God, and I keep my word.

XI
IT'S UP TO YOU!

I've been telling you over and over again that you have a choice between doing what's good for you and doing what hurts you. Whether or not you live the good life is up to you. No one else can make this decision for you.

I want the best for you, but I won't force you to choose the good life. I encourage you, however, to think carefully about what I've said. You may feel pressure from those around you to follow them instead of me. Use your head—don't just go along with the crowd!

Before people decide to construct a building, they figure out if they can afford it. They don't want to run out of money and regret that they ever started the project in the first place. It's even more important for you to think about the consequences of your own behavior! You don't want to regret your decisions, either. They determine what kind of life you live.

If you see the truth in what I'm telling you, and decide to live according to my guidelines, you'll be like a wise man who laid the foundation of his house on a rock. Rains fell, floods came, and strong winds blew—but the house stood firmly because it had been built on a rock. If, on the other hand, you ignore my words or reject them, you'll be like a foolish man who laid the foundation of his house on the sand. Rains fell, floods came, and strong winds blew—and the house collapsed because it had been built on sand.

I've been careful to explain the differences between what's good for you and what isn't, so you really don't have any excuse if you hurt yourself. You can't claim that you didn't know any better. That's why you may as well decide to follow me. You're capable of becoming a better, happier person this very minute. Why wait?

A farmer plows the ground before planting seed; you, too, must break up the hardness in your heart before goodness can grow there. Come to me, and I'll free you from your twisted thinking. Many people in the past were stubborn and rebellious; they refused to see the truth when it was right in front of their own eyes. They wouldn't keep my agreement—and they're long gone. Would you rather be like them, or like my servants, who live forever?

You keep putting off making a decision. What are you waiting for? How can you doubt for a second that I won't do what I say, or that I won't give you the good life? Do you think that I won't hear you if you call to me? The only way you'll ever find out is by trying.

So come to me now. Don't procrastinate any longer. Don't laugh at what I'm telling you. Listen to me—I know what's best for you. After all, I made you! There's no reason at all for you to be unhappy. You could be living the good life right now.

I'll tell you one more story to help you understand what I'm saying.

It's up to you!

A king decided to give a dinner in honor of his son's marriage. He invited many guests, and when everything was ready, he sent his servants out to tell the guests that it was time for the celebration. But none of the guests would come!

The servants returned to the king, and the king sent them out again with the same message. "Please come," the servants pleaded with the guests. "Don't keep the king waiting."

The guests started making excuses. "I just bought a new house," one said. "I have to take care of some last-minute details. I can't possibly come to dinner."

"I just bought a new car," said another. "I want to take it for a long drive to make sure that everything works."

"I just got married myself!" said a third. "I'm too busy, as you can imagine!"

Many people just laughed or shut their doors in the servants' faces. Some of them even mistreated the king's servants for bothering them. Needless to say, the king was furious when he heard about this. He gathered his servants around him again and said, "I still want to give a dinner in my son's honor, but don't bother anymore with the people who were originally invited to come. Instead, go out into the streets of the city and tell everyone you see about the celebration. Look especially for those who are poor, crippled, and blind. Invite as many of them as you can find."

The servants did what the king asked. Soon, people from all over the city were arriving. The servants looked around the dining hall, and went back to the king. "There's room for more," they said.

"Good!" answered the king. "Now go out into the country and invite anyone you meet. Look behind hedges and along roads that aren't traveled much. I want my house to be filled with guests."

The servants did what the king told them to do, and soon the king's house overflowed with happy people. But none of the guests who had originally been invited were there.

I'm like the king in the story—I invite you to come to me so I can give you the good life. Don't be like the ungrateful guests who made excuses. Accept my invitation now!

I've told you all about what'll happen to you if you decide to keep my agreement—and what'll happen to you if you don't. I've sent my messengers to you, and I've promised to give you all the help that you'll ever need to live according to my guidelines. I've done my part—now it's up to you!

Bible References

These references are to the *Oxford Annotated Bible*, Revised Standard Version. Each group of references is numbered; the numbers correspond to those found on the outside margin of the page in the text itself.

I I WANT TO MAKE AN AGREEMENT WITH YOU

   1 Ex. 3:7–9,16,17,19–22; 6:1,5; Lev. 26:13; Dt. 12:9; 1 Sam. 9:16; 2 Chr. 15:4; Is. 10:20; 41:17; 49:13; 51:21; 54:11; 55:1; Ezek. 20:5–6; Mt. 11:28; 19:26; Mk. 10:27; Lk. 18:27; Jn. 7:37; 8:32; 10:10; 14:6; 16:4–7.

Who I am
   2 Ex. 6:2,3,6,8,29; Lev. 19:28; 22:8,30; 25:38; 26:45; Dt. 7:9; Is. 30:15; 42:6; 43:10,11,13,15; 44:6,24; 48:12,17; 49:7; 54:8; Jer. 33:4; Ezek. 7:2; Hos. 12:5; Am. 5:27; Zeph. 3:15.
   3 Ex. 3:6,14,15; 4:5; Is. 40:28; 41:4; 44:6; 48:12,16; Jn. 8:58.
   4 Ex. 8:22; Dt. 4:39; 6:4; 10:17; Is. 5:9; 10:33; 18:7; 19:18; 22:5,12,14; 24:23; 28:5; 37:32; 43:10; 44:6,8; 45:5,13,18,21,22; 46:9; 47:4; 48:2; 51:15; 54:5; Jer. 6:9; 8:3; 19:3; 27:16,18,19,21; 29:17;

(139)

31:23; 32:27; 39:16; 42:15; 46:18; 48:1,15; Jer. 50:18,33,34; Hos. 12:5; Jl. 2:27; Am. 5:14, 27; 6:14; Hag. 2:23; Zech. 1:3,6; 3:7; 5:4; 6:12,15; 8:3,7; 9:15; 12:5; 14:16,17; Mal. 1:4,14; 2:4; 3:10; 4:3; Mk. 12:29; Jn. 17:3.

5 Gen. 17:1; 18:14; 35:11; Dt. 7:21; 10:17; 11:2; 2 Chr. 25:7-8 Is. 10:21; 40:15,16,26,28; 45:7; 60:16; Jer. 32:27; 50:34; Nah. 1:3; Mt. 19:26; Mk. 10:27; 14:36; Jn. 10:29.

6 Is. 57:15; 66:1,2; Jer. 23:23,24; Zech. 4:10.

7 Is. 40:15-17,21-22.

8 Ex. 33:19; Lev. 11:44,45; 19:2; 21:8; Jos. 24:19; Is. 10:17,20 12:6; 29:19,23; 30:15; 41:14, 16; 43:3,14,15; 47:4; 48:17; 49:7; 54:5; 57:15; 60:9,14; Hos. 11:12; Mt. 19:17; Mk. 10:18; Lk. 18:19; Jn. 17:11.

9 Is. 55:8-9; Hos. 11:9.

10 Dt. 10:17-18; Is. 5:16; 24:16; 30:18; 45:21; 61:8; Jer. 9:24; Hos. 14:9; Zeph. 3:5; Zech. 8:8; Mt. 5:45; Lk. 6:35; Jn. 17:25.

11 Is. 31:2; 40:13,14,28; 45:19; 65:16; Jn. 7:28; 8:26; 17:17.

12 Is. 28:24-29; 45:15.

13 Ex. 34:6,7; Dt. 1:34; 4:25,31; 6:15; 7:4,9; 9:7,8; 11:17; 29:27; 31:17,29; 1 Kg. 14:9; 2 Kg. 21:15; 2 Chr. 25:15; Is. 1:24; 5:25; 28:21 34:2,8; 47:3; 57:17; 65:3,5; Jer. 3:12; 8:19; 9:24; 11:17; 12:13; 25:6,7,37,38; 32:29, 30, 31,32; 44:3,8; 50:13,15; 51:11; Ezek. 8:17; 22:13; 25:17; Hos. 8:5; 12:14; Jl. 2:13; Jon. 4:11; Mic. 5:15; Nah. 1:2,3; Zech. 1:2; 8:14; Mt. 11:29; Jn. 17:24.

14 Is. 14:24,26,27; 43:13; 46:10,11; 55:10,11; Jer. 39:16; 51:29 Ezek. 21:7,17; 24:14; 26:5,14; 30:12; Mt. 24:34; Mk. 13:30; Lk. 21:32; Jn. 10:35.

15 Is. 40:6-8; Mt. 5:18; 24:35; Mk. 13:31; Lk. 16:17; 21:33.

I made the world good

16 Gen. 1; 8:17; 9:1,6,7; 35:11; Is. 40:12,22,26,28; 42:5; 44:2 45:12,18; 48:13; 51:13,16; Jer. 27:5; 33:2; Zech. 12:1.

Your responsibilities

17 Gen. 18:19; Ex. 15:26; Dt. 6:18; Dt. 12:25,28; 13:18; 1 Kg. 11:38; 14:8; Is. 1:17, 27; 3:10; 7:15,16; 11:5; 32:8; 33:15; 51:7; 53:11; 56:1; Jer. 4:2; 22:3,15; 23:5; 33:15; Ezek. 18:5,22; Hos. 10:12; 14:9; Am. 5:14,15; Mic. 2:7; Hab. 2:4; Mal. 2:6; Mt. 3:15; 5:6; 25:46; Lk. 6:21,35; Jn. 5:29.

18 Is. 7:15,16; 56:2; Ezek. 9:4; 18:8,17; Am. 5:14,15; Zeph. 3:13.

19 Gen. 26:5; Ex. 15:26; 20:6; 34:11; Lev. 7:36; 10:9; 17:7;

18:4,5,26; 19:19,37; 20:8; 20:22; 22:9,31; 23:21; 25:18; 26:3; Num. 15:40; 35:29; Dt. 4:1,2,5,6,40; 5:1, 10,29,32; 6:1, 2,3,17; 7:9, 11,12; 8:1,6; 10:13; 11:1,8,13,22,31,32; 12:1,28,32; 13:4,18; 15:5; 16:12; 19:9; 24:18; 15:15; 26:16,18; 27:1,10,26; 28:1,9,13; 29:29; 30:10,16; 31:12; Jos. 1:7; 1 Kg. 9:4; 11:38; 14:8; 2 Kg. 10:30; 17:37; 21:8; 2 Chr. 7:17; Is. 1:19; 51:7; 56:2; Jer. 2:31; 22:4; Ezek. 11:20; 18:9,17; 20:11,19; 37:24; Mt. 5:19;.7:21; 12:50; 19:17; Mk. 3:35; 10:19; Lk. 8:21; 10:28; 11:28; 18:20; Jn. 8:31, 51,55; 12:50; 13:17; 14:15; 15:10,14; 17:6.

20 Gen. 17:1; Dt. 4:2; 5:32,33; 8:6; 10:12,13; 11:22; 12:32; 13:4; 19:9; 28:9,14; 30:16; Jos. 1:7; 1 Kg. 11:38; 2 Chr. 7:17; Jer. 7:23; 26:4; 32:39; Ezek. 18:9, 17; Hos. 14:9; Mic. 2:7; Zech. 3:7; Mal. 2:6.

21 Dt. 30:11–14; Is. 43:23; Mic. 6:3; Mt. 11:30.

22 Gen. 17:2–8; 17:19; Ex. 6:3,4; 34:10,27; Num. 18:19; Dt. 4:31; 5:2,3; 7:9,12; 29:14,15; Jg. 2:1; 2 Kg. 17:35; Is. 55:3; 61:8; Jer. 32:40; 34:13,15; Ezek. 16:60,62; 37:26; Mal. 2:5.

23 Gen. 17:9; Ex. 19:5; Lev. 18:5; Num. 21:8; Dt. 4:1,23; 5:33; 16:20; 29:9; 30:6,16,19,20; 2 Kg. 17:38; Is. 55:3; 56:4,6; Jer. 11:3,4; 11:6; 27:17; Ezek. 18:9,21,22,32; 20:11,13,21; 37:5,6,9,14; Hos. 6:2; Am. 5:4,6,14; Hab. 2:4; Zech. 10:9; Mal. 2:4,5; Lk. 10:28; 21:19; Jn. 3:15,16; 5:40; 8:51; 10:28.

24 Ex. 28:35,43; 30:20,21; Lev. 16:2,13; 22:9; 26:38; Num. 4:20; 18:3; 20:12; 26:65; Dt. 4:26; 8:19,20; 11:17; 28:20,51; 29:20; 30:18; 2 Kg. 1:3,4; 2 Kg. 1:16; Is. 7:9; 22:18; 65:15; 66:17; Jer. 17:13; 22:12,26; 27:10; 42:16; 48:35; Ezek. 26:21; Nah. 1:14; Zeph. 3:2; Mk. 16:16; Lk. 13:3,5; Jn. 3:18; Jn. 8:21,24; 15:6.

25 Num. 16:38; Dt. 32:47; Is. 3:11; 5:8; 28:1; 29:15; 45:9,10; Jer. 7:6; 13:27; 25:7; 48:46; Ezek. 33:10; Hab. 2:10,19; Zeph. 2:5; 3:1; Lk. 6:26.

26 Gen. 2:16,17; 3:13; Ex. 32:33; Lev. 4:13,14,27; 5:14.17;15:24; Num. 15:25–29; Dt. 4:25; 9:12; 17:2; 31:29; 1 Kg. 14:9; 2 Kg. 21:11,15; 2 Chr. 21:12,13; Is. 1:4; 65:12; 66:4; Jer. 4:22; 6:28; 7:30; 11:15; 32:30; 44:9; 51:24; Ezek. 6:11; 8:6; 8:17; 14:7; 16:50; 18:12,13; 33:26; 45:20; Hos. 10:9,13; Mic. 1:5; Jn. 5:29.

27 Ex. 32:7; Is. 59:3; Jer. 2:22; Ezek. 20:30,31, 43; 22:4,24; 36:17; Nah. 1:14; Zeph. 3:1; Hag. 2:11–14.

28 Is. 1:4; 59:2; Jer. 5:25.

29 Gen. 17:14; Lev. 7:25,27; 17:4,9,10; 18:29; 19:8; 20:6; 23:29; Num. 9:13; 15:30,31; Dt. 29:21; 31:29; 1 Kg. 9:7,9; 1 Kg. 11:11; 2 Kg. 22:16; 2 Chr. 7:22; 34:24; Is. 29:20; 47:11; 48:9; Jer. 4:15; 6:18,19; 11:17,23; 18:11; 19:15; 21:10; 25:29; 35:17; 36:3,31; 39:16; 42:17; 44:2,8,11,27; 49:37; Ezek. 6:10; 14:8; 25:7,16; 30:15;

Am. 9:4; Ob. 9,10; Mic. 1:12; 2:3; Zech. 2:9; 5:3; 8:14; Mal. 2:12; Mt. 5:20; 21:43

You do it to yourself
  30 2 Kg. 21:13; Is. 3:13; 33:22; 41:1; Jer. 25:31; 51:36; Hos. 4:1; 12:2; Am. 7:8; Mic. 1:2; 6:1,2; Zeph. 3:8; Mal. 3:5; Jn. 8:50.
  31 Dt. 1:34; Is. 37:28; 57:18; 59:15; 66:18; Jer. 5:3; 6:7; 14:10; 16:17; 23:24; Ezek. 11:5; Hos. 5:3; 7:2; 8:13; 9:9; Am. 5:12; 8:7; 9:8; Mt. 6:4,6,18; Lk. 2:35.
  32 Mt. 10:26; Mk. 4:22; Lk. 8:17; 12:2,3.
  33 2 Chr. 15:7; Is. 3:10; 40:10; 61:8; 62:11; Jer. 31:16; Mt. 6:4,6,18; Lk. 6:35.
  34 Ex. 32:33,34; Dt. 7:10; 1 Sam. 8:8; Is. 3:11; 34:8; 59:18; 65:6,7; 66:6; Jer. 17:10; 21:14; 25:14; 50:29; 51:24,56; Ezek. 7:3,8,27; 9:10; 11:21; 16:59; 18:30; 22:31; 24:14; 33:20; 36:19; 39:24; Hos. 12:2; Jl. 3:4,7; Ob. 15; Zech 1:6.
  35 Ex. 28:43; 34:7; Lev. 4:27; 5:5,19; 6:7; Is. 13:9,11; 24:21,22; 26:21; 34:5; Jer. 2:9; 4:11,12; 5:9,29; 6:6,15; 9:9,25,26; 11:22,23; 14:10; 25:29; 27:8; 30:11,14,15; 36:31; 44:13; 46:21,25,26,28; 48:21–24,44; 49:8; 50:18,27; 51:5; Ezek. 5:10; 7:3,4,8,9; 9:9; 11:9; 14:21; 21:30; 22:4; 25:11; 30:14,19; Hos. 1:4; 5:1,2; 7:12; 8:13; 9:7,9; 10:4,10; Am. 1:3,6,9,11,13; 2:1; 3:2,13,14; Zeph. 1:9,12; Zech. 9:1,2; 14:19; Mk. 16:16; Jn. 3:18.
  36 Ex. 34:7; Lev. 5:7,11,17; 7:18; 16:34; 17:16; 19:8; 22:9; 26:39; Num. 9:13; 14:34; 15:31; Dt. 18:12; 28:20; 31:18; Is. 3:8,9; Jer. 2:17,19; 4:4,18; 6:19; 7:12,13; 11:17; 13:22; 15:13; 17:3; 21:12; 30:15; 33:5; 44:3,7; Ezek. 5:9; 7:13; 16:52,58; 18:13; 33:10,29; Mic. 1:5; 3:4; 6:13; 7:13; Hos. 9:15; 10:2,15; 12:14; 13:16; Zeph. 1:17.

It's your choice
  37 Ex. 20:5; 34:7; Lev. 26:39; Num. 14:33; Dt. 5:9; 28:46; Is. 14:21; 65:7; Jer. 16:12; 31:29,30; Ezek. 14:13–20; 18:2–4,10–20.

You need to become a new person
  38 Ex. 3:12,17,20; 6:1,6,7; 7:4; 19:3–6; 20:2; 29:46; 32:7; 33:1; Lev. 11:45; 19:36; 22:33; 25:38, 55; 26:13,45; Num. 15:41; Dt. 4:20,37; 5:6; 7:8,19; 11:3; 13:5; 20:1; 29:2,3,16,25; Jg. 2:1; 6:8,9; 1 Sam. 8:8; 10:18; 1 Kg. 9:9; 2 Kg. 17:36; 2 Chr. 6:5; 7:22; Is. 31:5; 50:8; 51:22; 54:17; 63:1; Jer. 11:4,7; 31:32; 34:13; 51:10; Ezek. 20:9; 33:24,25; 34:27; Hos. 11:1; 12:9; 13:4; Am. 2:10; 3:1; Mic. 6:4; Zech. 10:11; Mal. 3:7; Jn. 6:63.

Bible references (143)

39 Is. 43:11; Hos. 13:4; Mt. 7:13, 14; Mk. 10:24; Lk. 13:24–28; Jn. 10:9; 14:6.
40 Jn. 3:3–7.

II HOW TO BECOME A NEW PERSON

First, make things right with me
  1 Lev. 26:41; Dt. 10:16; 1 Kg. 21:29; 2 Kg. 22:19; 2 Chr. 7:14; 12:7; 34:27; Is. 1:27; 57:15; 66:2; Jer. 4:4; 31:19; Ezek. 14:6; 16:61,63; 18:30; 20:43; 36:31; Jl. 2:13; Mt. 3:2, 11; 4:17; 18:3,4; Mk. 1:15; 10:14,15; Lk. 13:3,5; 18:17.

  2 2 Kg. 22:19; 2 Chr. 34:27; Is. 1:29; 57:18; Jer. 22:22; 31:19; Ezek. 16:52, 54, 61,63; 20:43; 36:31,32; 43:10; Jl. 2:12.

  3 Ex. 29:36,37; 30:10,15,16; Lev. 1:4; 4:20,28,31,35; 5:6,10,13,16,18; 6:7; 12:7,8; 14:18–21,29,31; 14:53; 15:15,30; 16:6,10,11,16,18,24,30,32–34; 17:11; 23:28; Num. 5:8; 8:12, 19; 15:25,27,28; 28:22, 30; 29:5,11; Is. 27:5; 51:1; Ezek. 43:20, 26; 45:15,17,20.

  4 Lev. 5:5; 16:21; 26:40; Num. 5:7; Dt. 4:29; 26:17,18; 2 Chr. 7:14; 15:2,4; 19:3; Is. 12:4; 51:1; 55:6; 58:9; 59:12; 65:10; Jer. 3:13; 29:12,13; 33:3; 50:4; Hos. 3:5; 14:2,3; Jl. 1:14; 2:32; Am. 5:4,6; Zeph. 3:9; Zech. 13:9.

Next, make things right with other people
  5 Lev. 5:16; 6:1–7; 26:41,43; Num. 5:7,8.

I forgive you
  6 Lk. 15:11–32.

  7 Gen. 4:7; Ex. 20:24; Lev. 23:11; Dt. 4:30; 30:2,10; 2 Chr. 15:4; Is. 30:15; 31:6; 35:4; 40:9; 41:9; 44:22; 45:22; 55:7; 66:2; Jer. 3:12,14; 4:1; 15:19; 24:7; 31:21; Exek. 18:32; 20:40,41; 36:9; 43:27; Hos. 3:5; 6:1,3; 14:1,2; Jl. 2:12,13; Zech. 1:3,16; 2:10; 8:3; 9:12; Mal. 3:4, 7; Jn. 6:37; 14:18,23,25,28,29.

  8 Ex. 34:7; Lev. 4:20,31,35; 5:10,13,16,18; 6:7; Num 14:20; 15:25,28; 19:9; Dt. 21:9; 2 Chr. 7:14; Is. 33:24; 40:2; 43:25; 44:22; 55:7; Jer. 31:34; 33:8; 36:3; Ezek. 16:63; 18:22; Mt. 6:14; 12:31,32; Mk. 3:28; 11:25; Lk. 6:37; 12:10.

  9 Lev. 12:7,8; 14:20,53; 16:30; Is. 1:16,18; 4:4; 27:9; 52:1,2,11; 61:10; Jer. 4:14; 33:8; Ezek. 36:25,33; 37:23; Zech. 3:4,5,9,10; Mt. 8:3; Mk. 1:41; Lk. 5:13; Jn. 13:8,10; 15:3.

  10 Is. 42:1; Zeph. 3:17; Mt. 18:12,18; Lk. 15:3–10.

You're a new person

11 Lev. 26:13; Is. 9:4; 10:27; 14:25; 51:14; Jer. 30:8; Ezek. 34:27; Hos. 11:4; Nah. 1:13; Zech. 9:11; Lk. 13:12; Jn. 8:31,36.

12 Ex. 3:8; 6:6; Dt. 7:8; 13:5; 23:14; Jg. 6:9; 1 Sam. 10:18; 2 Kg. 19:34; Is. 1:27; 12:2; 25:9; 29:22; 30:15; 31:5; 33:22; 35:4,10; 37:35; 41:14; 43:1,3,12,14; 44:6,22,24; 45:15,21,22; 46:4,13; 47:4; 48:17,20; 49:7,8; 51:5,6,8,11; 52:3,9; 54:5,8; 56:1; 59:20; 60:16; 61:10; 62:11,12; 63:1,4; Jer. 3:23; 4:14; 15:20,21; 30:11; 31:7,11; 39:17,18; 42:11; 50:34; Exek. 34:27; 36:29; 37:23; Hos. 1:7; 10:12; Jl. 2:32; Mic. 4:10; 6:4; Zeph. 3:19; Zech. 8:7,13; 9:16; 10:6,8; Mt. 10:22; 24:13; Mk. 13:13; 16:16; Lk. 19:9; Jn. 4:22; 10:9.

13 Dt. 12:8; 2 Chr. 7:14; Is. 1:16; 55:7; 59:20; Jer. 7:3,5; 18:11; 25:5; 26:13; 36:3; Exek. 14:6,11; 18:30,31; 33:11; Mt. 11:29; Jn. 5:14; 8:11.

14 Lev. 26;11; Num. 18:5; 25:4; Dt. 4:31; 13:17; Is. 12:1; 31:5; 54:9; 57:16; Jer. 3:12; 25:6; 26:13; 42:10; Hos. 14:4; Jl. 2:13,14; Nah. 1:12; Zeph. 3:15; Zech. 8:11; Mal. 3:17; Jn. 3:18; 5:24; 8:11.

15 Ex. 33:19; Dt. 23:5; Jer. 17:13; 18:1–6; 29:11; 31:17; 32:40,41,42; Ezek. 36:11; Zech. 8:15; 10:6; Jn. 5:24.

What happens if you turn away from me again?

16 Jer. 2:3; 11:16; Hos. 9:10.

17 Lev. 26:14,15,43; Num. 15:22,23,31; Dt. 11:28; 28:15,47,58; Jos. 7:15; Jg. 2:2; 1 Sam. 15:11; 1 Kg. 11:11,33; 1 Kg. 13:21; 2 Chr. 24:20; Is. 1:22; 24:5; 42:24; Jer 2:19; 6:16,19; 11:8; 16:11; 44:10; 48:10; Ezek. 5:6,7; 11:12; Hos. 7:8; 8:1; Mic. 5:15; Hab. 2:4; Zeph. 1:6; Mal. 3:5,7; Jn. 7:19.

18 Num. 5:6; 11:20; 1 Sam. 15:23; Is. 5:24; Jer. 15:6; 18:13,14.

19 Is. 1:2; 30:9; Jer. 3:19; Hos. 7:15; 11:1,3,4.

20 Num. 20:24; 27:14; Dt. 9:7, 12; Jos. 7:11; Jg. 2:2; 1 Sam. 15:23; 1 Kg. 9:6; Is. 1:2,20; 31:6; 48:8; 66:24; Jer. 2:20,29,31; 3:13; 4:17; 11:9,10; Ezek. 18:11; 20:13,16,21,24; Hos. 7:13,14; 13:5,16; Am. 2:4; Zeph. 3:1.

21 Ex. 32:8; Dt. 28:20; 29:25; 31:16,29; 1 Sam. 8:8; 1 Kg. 9:9; 11:33; 14:9; 2 Kg. 22:17; 2 Chr. 7:19,22; 15:2; 24:20; 34:25; Is. 1:4,28; 65:11; Jer. 2:12,13,17,19,27; 5:7,19,23; 6:8; 9:13; 16:11; 17:5,13; 19:4; 22:9; 32:33; 42:19,20; Ezek. 14:7; Hos. 1:2; 7:13; 11:7.

22 Gen. 17:14; Lev. 26:15; Dt. 17:2; Jos. 7:11; Jg. 2:20; Is. 24:5; Jer. 11:10; 31:32; 34:18; Ezek. 17:2–10; 18:18; 44:7; Hos. 6:7; 8:1,3; Mal. 2:10.

23 Ezek. 28:12–19.

24 Jer. 18:7–10; Ezek. 18:21,24,25; 33:12–19.
25 Mt. 12:43–45; Lk. 11:24–26.

What my guidelines are
26 Ex. 35:1; Dt. 5:28,29; 6:4,5; 10:12; Jer. 4:1; 17:21; Ezek. 44:6; Mic. 6:8; Zech. 8:16; Mt. 19:17; 22:37–40; Mk. 12:29–31; Lk. 10:27,28.

III HOW TO LOVE ME

Remember that I'm the only true God
1 Ex. 20:5; 34:14; Dt. 4:24; 5:9; 6:15; Jos. 24:19; Is. 42:8; 48:11; Ezek. 5:13; 36:5,6; Hos. 14:8; Jl. 2:18; Nah. 1:2; Zech. 1:14; 8:2.

2 Mt. 6:24; Lk. 16:13.

3 Ex. 20:3,5; 22:20; 23:13; 34:24; Lev. 19:4; 26:1; Dt. 5:7,9; 6:13; 26:10; 28:14; Jos. 24:14,23; 2 Kg. 17:35,36,37,38; Is. 30:22; 31:7; 43:12; Jer. 2:25; 7:6; 25:6; Ezek. 11:18; 18:6,15; 20:7; Hos. 4:15; 13:4; Am. 5:5; Lk. 4:8.

4 Ex. 20:4,23; 34:17; Lev. 19:4; 26:1; Dt. 4:15–18,23,25; 5:8,9; 16:21,22; 27:15.

5 Is. 40:25; 41:21–24,26–28,29; 44:7; 45:21; Jer. 3:23; 10:5.

6 Is. 40:18–20; 41:7; 44:12–20; 46:5–7; Hos. 8:5; Jer. 10:3,4; 10:5; Hab. 2:18,19.

7 Lev. 17:7.

8 Dt. 4:19; 17:3; Jer. 10:2.

9 Jn. 4:21–24.

10 Ex. 20:24–26.

11 Lev. 15:31; 19:30; 26:2; Dt. 23:1–8; Is. 56:7; Jer. 7:11,30; 32:34; Ezek. 5:11; 8:6; 43:7–9; 44:5,7–9; Mt. 21:13; Mk. 11:17; Lk. 19:46; Jn. 2:16.

12 Dt. 23:17,18.

Love me completely
13 Ex. 20:6; Dt. 5:10; 6:4,5; Dt. 7:9; 10:12,20; 11:1,13,22; 13:4; 19:9; 30:16,20; 2 Chr. 16:8; Is. 7:4,11; 10:20; 12:2; 25:9; 27:5; 30:15,18; 40:31; 49:23; 50:10; 56:6; 57:13; Jer. 17:7; 39:18; Ezek. 40:4; 44:5; Hos. 6:6; 11:12 12:6; Zeph. 3:8,12,13; Mal. 3:10; Mt. 22:37; Mk. 12:29,30; Lk. 10:27,28; Jn 16:27.

14 Ex. 19:6; 22:31; Lev. 11:44; 20:7; Jos. 3:5; 7:13; Is. 13:3; Mt. 13:44–46; Jn. 10:36.

(146)   *"Hello I'm God & I'm here to help you"*

    15 2 Chr. 15:2; Is. 11:1; Jer. 23:5; 33:15; Hos 14:8; Zech. 3:8; 6:12; Jn. 15:4,5,7–10,16.

    16 Jn. 6:53,54,56–58; 10:30,38; 14:9–11,20; 17:21,23,26.

Be my servant

    17 Is. 56:2; Ezek. 2:1,3,6,8; 3:1,10; 4:1,16; 7:2; 8:5–18; 11:15; 12:2,3,9,18; 14:13; 17:2; 20:46; 21:2,6,9,14,19; 22:18; 24:2,25; 33:24,30; 39:17; 40:4; 43:18; 44:5; 47:6; Mt. 8:20: 10:23; 12:8; 13:37,41; 16:27; 17:9,12,22; 20:18,28; 24:27,30; 25:31; 26:2,24,45,64; Mk. 9:12,31; 10:33,45; 13:26; 14:21,41,62; Lk. 9:22,44,58; 11:30; 17:24; 18:8,31; 19:10; 21:27; 24:7; Jn. 1:51; 3:14,17; 5:19,20,23; 8:28; 9:35.

    18 Is. 43:1,7,15,21; 44:2,21,24; 46:3,4; 49:1,5.

    19 Lev. 25:55: Is. 41:8,9; 42:1; 43:10; 44:1,2,21,26,28; 45:4; 48:20; 49:3,6; 52:13; 53:11; 54:17; 56:6; 65:13,15; 66:14; Jer. 46:27,28; 30:10; Ezek. 28:25; 34:23,24: 37:24,25; Hag. 2:23; Zech. 3:8; Jn. 12:26.

    20 Is. 11:10; 42:6; 43:10,12; 44:8; 45:1; 49:8; 55:3,4; 61:1; 66:19; Ezek. 12:3–6; 24:24,27; Mt. 26:64; 27:11; Mk. 14:62; 15:2; Lk. 4:18; 22:70; 23:3; 24:48; Jn. 3:16; 4:26; 8:14; 9:37; 13:19; 15:27; 18:5,8,37.

    21 Is. 41:9; 42:6; 48:12,15.

    22 Is. 42:6; 49:6; 51:4; 60:1; 62:1; Hos. 6:5; Mt. 5:14–16; Mk. 4:21; Lk. 2:32; 8:16; 11:33; Jn. 3:14; 8:12; 9:5; 12:46.

    23 Mt. 5:13; Mk. 9:50; Lk. 14:34,35.

    24 1 Sam. 2:35; Is. 44:28; 53:10; 56:4; Mt. 26:39; Mk. 14:36; Lk. 22:42; Jn. 4:32,34; 5:17,19,30,36; 6:38; 8:29; 10:32; 14:28; 17:4.

    25 Gen. 22:18; 26:5; Ex. 15:26; 19:5; 23:22; Dt. 4:30; 6:4; 13:4,18; 15:5; 27:10; 28:1,2; 30:2,10,20; 31:12; Jos. 24:23; 1 Kg. 11:38; Is. 7:13; 28:14,23; 32:9; 33:13; 34:1; 42:23; 44:1; 46:3,12; 48:12,14,16,18; 49:1; 51:1,4,21; 55:2,3; 66:5; Jer. 7:23; 11:4,6,7; 17:24; 26:13; 29:20; 35:13; Ezek. 3:10; 40:4; 44:5; Hos. 4:1; Mic. 6:9; Zech. 6:15; Mt. 7:24; 11:15,29; 13:43; 15:10; Mk. 4:23,24; Mk. 7:14; 12:29; Lk. 6:47; 8:18,21; 11:28; 14:35; Jn. 5:24,25; 14:31.

    26 Hos. 6:3,6; Mt. 15:10; Mk. 4:24–25; 7:14; Jn. 7:29; 8:55; 10:15; 17:3.

    27 Ex. 3:12; 23:25; Num. 14:24; Dt. 1:36; 6:13; 10:12,20; 11:13; 13:4; Jos. 24:14; 1 Kg. 14:8; Is. 56:6; Jer. 3:14; Mt. 4:19; 8:22; 9:9; 16:24; 19:21,28; Mk. 1:17; 2:14; 8:34; 10:21; Lk. 9:23,59; 14:27; 18:22; Jn. 1:43; 8:12; 10:27; 12:26; 21:19,22.

    28 Gen 17:1; Lev. 11:44,45; 18:24; 19:2; 10:26; Num. 5:3; 15:40; Dt. 7:6; 13:2; 14:21; 18:13; 23:14; 26:19; 28:9; 2 Chr. 16:9; Is.

62:12; Ob. 17; Mt. 5:8,20,45,48; Lk. 6:35; 10:6; Jn. 8:19,39–47; 14:7.

29 Dt. 12:7,12,18; 16:11; 26:11; 27:7; 28:47; Is. 25:9; 52:9; Jer. 31:16; Jl. 2:21, 23; Zeph. 3:14; Zech 2:10; Jn. 16:33.

Fight what's wrong

30 Dt. 1:42; Zech. 4:6; Lk. 24:49.

31 Gen. 4:7; Ex. 23:31,33; Num. 21:34; 33:51,52; Dt. 2:24; 3:2; 7:2,16,24; 9:3; 12:2,29; 20:16,17; 23:9; 24:7; 25:19; 31:5; Jos. 6:2–5; 8:1,2; 11:6; Jg. 4:6; 1 Sam. 15:3, 18; 1 Kg. 20:14; 2 Chr. 20:16,17; Is. 58:6; Ezek. 9:5; Mic. 4:13; 5:5,6; Mt. 10:8; Mk. 1:25; 7:27,29,30; 9:25; Lk. 4:35; 13:32.

32 Ex. 23:24; 34:13; Num. 33:52; Dt. 7:5,25; 12:2–4; Jg. 2:2; 2 Chr. 19:3; Is. 27:9.

33 Lev. 27:28,29; Is. 11:13,14; Mic. 4:13.

34 Dt. 7:17–24; 9:1,2; 20:1–4; Jos. 1:9; 8:1; 10:8; 2 Chr. 20:15,17; Is. 7:4; 8:6,12; 12:2; 40:9; 41:10,14; 43:1,5; 44:2; 54:4; Jer. 30:10; 46:27,28; Jl. 2:21; Zeph. 3:16; Hag. 2:5; Zech. 8:15; Mt. 1:20; 8:26; 14:27; 17:5,7; 24:6; 28:10; Mk. 6:50; 13:7; Lk. 1:13; 2:10; 5:10; 12:32; 21:9; Jn. 6:20; 14:1,27.

35 Num. 21:34; Dt. 3:2; 7:21; 31:6; Jos. 11:6; Is. 2:22; 10:20; 51:12; Ezek. 3:9; Mt. 10:26,28–31; Lk. 12:4–7.

36 Dt. 31:6; Jos. 1:6,7,9; 2 Chr. 15:7; Is. 35:4; 50:7; Zeph. 3:16; Hag. 2:4; Zech. 8:9,13; Mt. 7:7,8; Lk. 11:9,10.

37 Jer. 12:5; Mt. 7:6; 10:16.

Pray to me

38 Mt. 7:7,8,11; Lk. 11:9,10; Jn. 15:7.

39 Mt. 5:23,24; Mk. 11:25.

40 Mt. 6:5,6.

41 Jn. 14:12–14; 15:16; 16:23–24,26.

42 Hab. 2:4; Mt. 8:7,10,13; 9:22,28,29,30; 14:31; 15:28; 17:20; 21:19,21,22; Mk. 4:40; 5:30,34; 9:23; 10:52; 11:22–26; Lk. 7:9,50; 8:25,48; 17:6,19; 18:42; 23:46; Jn. 20:27,29.

43 Is. 53:12; 62:6,7; Jl. 2:17; Jn. 16:26; 17:9.

44 Mt. 6:7–15; Lk. 11:2–4.

Keep the Sabbath

45 Ex. 20:8–11; 23:12; 34:21; 35:2,3; Lev. 19:3,30; 23:2,3: 26:2; Dt. 5:12–15; Is. 56:2,4,6; Ezek. 20:13,21; 22:8.

46 Mt. 12:3–8; 11,12; Mk. 2:25–28; 3:4,5; Lk. 6:3–5,8–10; 13:15,16; 14:5; Jn. 7:22,23.

47 Ex. 16:23,28,29; Is. 58:13; Jer. 17:21,22,24,27.
48 Ex. 31:12–17; Ezek. 20:12,20.

Don't be a hypocrite

49 Ex. 20:7; Lev. 19:12; Dt. 5:11; Hos. 4:15; Mal. 1:12.
50 Lev. 22:32; Ezek. 39:25.
51 2 Kg. 19:34; Is. 37:35; 48:9,11; Ezek. 20:8–22,44; 22:16; 36:20–23,32; 39:27; Mal.3:6.
52 Mal. 2:2; Mt. 23:3,14; 24:51; Mk. 12:40; Lk. 20:47.
53 Mt. 23:25–28; Lk. 11:39–41,44.
54 Mt. 16:2,3; Lk. 12:54–56.
55 Mt. 23:29–36; Lk. 11:47,48.
56 Mt. 23:5–7; Mk. 12:38,39; Lk. 11:43,46.
57 Lev. 19:8 Ezek. 22:26; Mt. 23:4,13,15; Lk. 11:46,52.
58 Mt. 23:16–22.
59 Mt. 21:32; Mt. 23:23,24; Lk. 11:42.
60 Mt. 16:6,8–11; 23:2,3; Mk. 8:15,17–21; 12:38; Lk. 12:1; 20:46.
61 Lev. 19:14,32; 25:17,36; Dt. 4:10; 5:29; 6:2,13; 8:6; 10:12,20; 13:4; 14:23; 28:58; 31:12; Jos. 24:14; 2 Kg. 17:36, 39; Is. 11:3; 8:13; 33:6; 50:10; Jer. 5:22; 32:39; Mal. 2:5; 3:16; 4:2; Mic. 6:9.
62 Ex. 22:28; Lev. 22:10–16; 24:14–16; Num. 17:2–5,10; Dt. 6:16; Is. 8:13; 66:2,5; Hab. 2:20; Zeph. 1:7; Zech. 2:13; Mt. 4:7; Lk. 4:12.
63 Mt. 6:1,16–18.
64 Lev. 5:4; Num. 30: 1–15; Dt. 6:13; 10:20; 23:21–23; Nah. 1:15; Mt. 5:33–37.

Be humble

65 Mic. 2:3; 6:8; Zech. 9:9; Mt. 5:3,5; Lk. 6:20; 9:48.
66 Mt. 23:11,12; Lk. 18:10–14.
67 Mt. 23:8–10.
68 Lk. 14:8–11.
69 Dt. 7:7,8; 9:4–6.
70 Dt. 5:15; 15:15; 16:3,12; 24:18,22.
71 Jer. 9:23,24; Lk. 10:20.
72 Lk. 17:7–10.

Don't try to buy the good life

73 Mt. 6:19–21; Jn. 6:27.
74 Lk. 12:16–21.
75 Mt. 19:23,24; Mk. 10:23,25; Lk. 18:24,25.

Bible references

76 Mt. 19:21; Mk. 10:21; Lk. 12:33,34; 18:22.
77 Mt. 6:25–33; Lk. 10:41,42; 12:22–31.
78 Mt. 6:34.
79 Ex. 19:5,6; Lev. 25:23; Dt. 10:14; 12:21; Is. 66:2; Jn. 17:7.
80 Lk. 16:1–9.
81 Lk. 12:48.
82 Mt. 25:14–30; Lk. 19:12–27.
83 Mt. 25:29; Mk. 4:25; Lk. 8:18.

Give me tithes and offerings

84 Ex. 23:15; 25:2; 34:20; Num. 28:2; Dt. 12:6,11; 14:22–26; 16:10,16,17; Mal. 3:10.
85 Mk. 12:43,44; Lk. 21:3,4.
86 Ex. 12:5; 22:29; 23:19; 28:38; 29:1,18,41; 34:26; Lev. 1:3,9,10,13,17; 2:2,9; 3:1,5,6,16; 4:28,31,32; 5:15,18; 6:6,15,21; 14:10; 17:6; 19:5; 22:19–25,29; 23:10,12,13,14,18; Num. 15:3,7,10,13,14,17–21,24; 18:17; 28:2,3,6,8,11,13,24,27,31; 29:2,6,8,13,17,20,23,26,29,32,35,36; Dt. 17:1; 15:21; 18:4; 26:1–4; Ezek. 43:22,23,25; 44:30; 45:18,23; 46:4,6,13.
87 Lev. 27:2–33; Num. 6:2–21; Dt. 12:17,18; Is. 43:23,24; Jl. 1:13; Mal. 1:6–14; 3:8,9.
88 Dt. 26:5–11.
89 Dt. 14:28,29; 26:12; Mt. 5:42; 7:2; Lk. 6:30,38.
90 Mt. 6:2–4.
91 Dt. 26:12–15.

Take good care of the earth and its creatures

92 Gen. 9:2; Lev. 18:26, 27; 22:27,28; Num. 35:33, 34; Dt. 20:19,20; 22:6,7.
93 Ex. 23:4,5; Dt. 22:1–4; 25:4.
94 Lev. 19:9,10; 23:22; Dt. 23:24,25; 24:19–22.
95 Ex. 23:10,11; Lev. 19:19, 23–25; 25:2–7; Dt. 22:9,10,11.

Take good care of yourself

96 Ex. 29:4; 30:17–21; Lev. 1:9,13; 5:3; 7:19–21; 10:10; 15:31; 16:4,23,24,26,28; Num. 8:7; 18:11, 13; 19:20–22; Is. 52:11; Ezek. 43:20,22; 45:18.
97 Lev. 12:2–5; 15:1–28; 18:19; 20:18; 22:4; Num. 5:2,3; Dt. 23:10,11; Ezek. 18:6.
98 Gen. 17:9–14; Lev. 12:3; Dt. 23:12,13; Jos. 5:2.
99 Num. 5:2,3; 9:10; 19:11–19.
100 Lev. 13:1–46; 14:1–9; Num. 5:2,3; Dt. 24:8,9.

101 Lev. 13:47–58; 14:33–53.
102 Gen. 1:29,30; 9:3; Lev. 20:25.
103 Lev. 7:19; 11:2–8,24–28; Dt. 12:15,20; 14:3–8.
104 Ex. 23:19; 34:26; Dt. 14:21.
105 Gen. 9:3,4; Lev. 3:17; 7:22–27; 17:10–14; 19:26; Dt. 12:16, 23–25; 15:23.
106 Ex. 22:31; Lev. 11:39,40; 17:14–16; 22:8; Dt. 14:21.
107 Lev. 11:20–23.
108 Lev. 11:29–31, 41–45.
109 Lev. 11:13–19; Dt. 14:11–20.
110 Lev. 11:9–12; Dt. 14:9,10.
111 Lev. 5:2; 11:32–38.

IV HOW TO LOVE OTHER PEOPLE

Love others as you love yourself

1 Lev. 19:18; Is. 11:5; Hos. 10:12; 12:6; Mic. 6:8; Zech. 7:9; 8:19; Mt. 5:7,9; 9:13; 12:7; 15:32; 19:19; 22:39; Mk. 8:2; 9:50; 12:31; Lk. 6:36; 10:27; Jn. 13:14, 34; 15:12,13,17; 17:26.

2 Lk. 10:30–37.

3 Mal. 2:10; Mt. 5:43–48; 7:12; 18:10; Lk. 6:27,28,31–35; Jn. 13:35; 17:11,21,22,23.

Be forgiving

4 Is. 58:9; Mt. 7:1–5; Lk. 6:37,42,42; Jn. 8:7,10,11.

5 Lev. 19:17,18; 25:17; Dt. 23:7; Ezek. 18:16; Zech. 7:10; 8:17; Mt. 5:21,22,38–41; Lk. 6:29.

6 Lev. 19:17; Mt. 6:14,15; 18:22; Lk. 6:37; 17:3,4.

7 Mt. 18:23–35.

8 Mt. 5:25,26; 18:15–18; Lk. 12:57–59.

Lend to people in need

9 Ex. 22:25; Dt. 15:7,8,10,11; Ezek. 18:8, 17; Mt. 5:42; Lk. 6:34,35.

10 Lev. 25:35–37; Dt. 15:1–3,9; 23:19,20.

11 Ex. 22:25–27; Dt. 24:6,10–13,17; Ezek. 18:7,16.

Help those less fortunate than you

12 Ex. 22:24; Lev. 19:13,14; Dt. 27:18; Is. 42:3; Jer. 7:6; 22:3; Ezek. 18:7; Zech. 7:10.

13 Is. 1:17; 28:12; 33:15; 35:3; 58:6,7,9,10; 61:1,2,3; Jer. 21:12; 22:3; Ezek. 16:54; 18:7,16; Mt. 10:8; 14:16,18; 15:32,34; 25:35–40; Mk. 6:31,37,38; 7:34; 8:2,3,5; Lk. 9:13, 14; 10:9; 13:32,33; Jn. 6:5,10,12.

Bible references (151)

14 Ex. 22:21; 23:9; Lev. 19:33,34; Dt. 10:19; Mt. 25:35.
15 Lk. 14:12–14.

Do what's just

16 Gen. 18:19; Dt. 16:18,20; Is. 1:17,27; 42:1,3,4; 56:1; 61:8; Jer. 5:1; 7:5; 21:12; 22:3,15; 33:15; Hos. 12:6; Am. 5:24; Mic. 6:8.
17 Ex. 23:3,6; Lev. 19:15,35; Dt. 16:19; 24:17; 27:19; Is. 1:17; 11:3,4; Jer. 22:16; Ezek. 18:8; Am. 5:15; Zech. 7:9; 8:16; Jn. 7:24.
18 Ex. 23:8; Dt. 16:19; 27:25; Is. 33:15.
19 Ex. 12:49; Lev. 24:22; Num. 9:14; 15:15,16.
20 Dt. 24:16; 2 Kg. 14:6; 2 Chr. 25:4.
21 Ex. 21:23–25; Lev. 24:19,20; Dt. 25:1–3.
22 Num. 35:30; Dt. 19:15.

Tell the truth

23 Ex. 20:16; 23:1,2,7; Lev. 5:1; 19:11,16; Dt. 5:20; 19:16–21; Is. 53:9; 58:9; Jer. 4:2; 5:1; Zeph. 3:13; Zech. 8:16,17,19; Mal. 2:6; Mt. 19:18; Mk. 10:19; Lk. 18:20.

Don't covet or steal

24 Ex. 20:17; Dt. 5:21; Lk. 12:15.
25 Ex. 20:15; Lev. 19:11,13; Dt. 5:19; Is. 61:8; Ezek. 18:7, 16; Mt. 19:18; Mk. 10:19; Lk. 6:30; 18:20.
26 Lk. 16:10–12.
27 Lev. 19:35,36; Dt. 25:13,-16; Ezek. 45:10–12.
28 Lev. 25:13–17,23–34; Dt. 19:14; 27:17.
29 Ex. 22:1,4–15.

Don't murder

30 Ex. 20:13; Lev. 19:16; Dt. 5:17; 27:24; Is. 33:15; 53:9; Jer. 7:6; 22:3; Mt. 19:18; Mk. 10:19; Lk. 18:20.
31 Gen. 9:5,6; Lev. 24:17,21; Num. 35:33.
32 Ex. 21:12–14; Num. 35:16–28; Dt. 19:4–13.
33 Num. 35:10–15,31,32; Dt. 17:6–13; 19:1–3; Jos. 20:1–6.
34 Ex. 21:18,19,22,28–36; 22:2,3; Lev. 24:18,21; Dt. 21:22,23; 22:8; 25:11,12.

Choose leaders who keep my agreement

35 Ex. 22:28; Lev. 4:1–12; Dt. 17:14–20; Ezek. 45:8,9; 46:16–18; Mt. 20:25–28; 23:11; Mk. 9:33,35; 10:42–45; Lk. 22:25–27.

Be responsible in sexual relationships and in marriage

36 Lev. 18:22; 20:13; Dt. 22:5; 23:18.
37 Ex. 22:19; Lev. 18:23; 20:15,16; Dt. 27:21.

38 Lev. 18:6–17; 20:11,12,17,19,20,21; Dt. 22:30;27:20,22,23.
39 Ex. 20:14; Dt. 5:18; Mt. 5: 27, 28; 19:18; Mk. 10:19; Lk. 18:20.
40 Lev. 18:20; 20:10; Dt. 22:22; Ezek. 18:6,15.
41 Mal. 2:15; Mt. 19:4–6; Mk. 10:5–9.
42 Mt. 19:11,12; Jer. 29:6.
43 Mal. 2:11.
44 Lev. 18:18; 20:14.
45 Dt. 24:5.
46 Mal. 2:14–16.
47 Mal. 2:16; Mt. 5:31,32; 19:8,9; Mk. 10:11,12; Lk. 16:18.
48 Num. 5:12–31; Dt. 24:1–4.
49 Ex. 22:16,17; Lev. 19:20–22; Dt. 22:13–29.

Care for your parents and children
50 Ex. 20:12; 21:15,17; Lev. 19:3; 20:9; Dt. 5:16; 27:16; Is. 58:7; Mt. 19:19; Mk. 10:19; Lk. 18:20; Jn. 19:26,27.
51 Lev. 19:27,28,32; Dt. 14:1.
52 Gen. 18:19; Dt. 1:39; 4:9,10; 6:2,7; 11;19; 31:13; 32:46; Is. 7:15,16; Jl. 1:2,3.
53 Ex. 10:2; Dt. 6:20–25.
54 Mt. 18:5; 19:14; Mk. 9:37; 10:14; Lk. 9:48; 18:16.
55 Lev. 18:21; 20:2–5; Dt. 12:31;.18:10,12.
56 Lev. 19:29; 21;9.
57 Dt. 21:15–17.
58 Dt. 21:18–21.

Be kind to the people who work for you
59 Ex. 21:1–11,16,20,21,26,27; Lev. 19:13; 25:39–54; Dt. 15:12–18; 23:15,16; 24:7,14,15; Jer. 34:14–17.

V HOW TO TELL OTHER PEOPLE ABOUT ME

Who my prophets were
1 Num. 4:19; Ezek. 18:23,32; 33:11; Jon. 4:10,11; Mt. 18:14; Jn. 3:16; 17:21.
2 Is. 59:16,17; 63:3,5; Ezek. 22:30.
3 Num. 12:6–8; Is. 44:7,8; 45:19; 46: 8–11; 48:3–5,16; Ezek. 38:17; Hos. 12:10,13; Am. 2:11; 3:3–8; Zech. 7:12; 8:9; Mt. 11:13.
4 Num. 25:11–13; Jg. 6:7,8; 2 Kg. 17:13; 2 Chr. 25:15; Is. 21:6–10; Jer. 7:25,26; 35:14,15; 44:4; Ezek. 4:1–3; Mic. 6:4.
5 Ex. 23:20,21; Dt. 18:15–19; Is. 28:16; 43:10; 50:10; Mt. 11:6; Mk. 1:15; 5:36; 9:23; 16:16,17; Lk. 7:23; 8:50; Jn. 3:18;

Bible references (153)

5:23,24; 6:29,35,40,47; 7:38; 8:24,42; 11:15, 25,26,40; 12:46; 13:19; 14:1,12,29; 16:17.
    6 Is. 6:8.

Speak my words

    7 Is. 44:26; 62:6; Jer. 6:27; 15:19; Ezek. 3:17; 33:7; Mal. 3:1.
    8 Ezek. 3:18–21; 33:2–9.
    9 Is. 42:2; 62:1; Jer. 5:1; Jl. 2:15,16; Mt. 10:32,33; Mk. 8:38; Lk. 9:26; 12:8,9.
    10 Is. 40:9; Jer. 11:6; 16:10; 25;30; 31:10–14; Ezek. 2:7; 3:4,11,17; 33:7; 40:4; Jon. 1:2; 3:2; Mt. 10:27.
    11 Jer. 30:2; 36:2; Hab. 2:2.
    12 Ezek. 2:5; 3:27; 33:33; Jn. 10:25.

Go to the world

    13 Is. 45:8; 49:6; Lk. 2:30,31; Jn. 10:10.
    14 Ex. 4:12; Is. 12:4,5; 42:4, 21; 45:6; 51:4,5; Jer. 2:2; 3:12; Ezek. 3:1,4,11; Mt. 28:19; Mk. 16:15; Lk. 4:43.
    15 Is. 40:3,4; 62:10; Mal. 3:1; Mt. 11:7–10; Lk. 7:24–27; Jn. 1:23; 3:28.
    16 Is. 61:1; Mt. 9:12,13; 11:5; 15:24; Mk. 2:17; Lk. 4:18; 5:31–32; 7:22; 19:10.
    17 Ex. 3:10; 4:2–9, 12–17,19,21–23; 6:11,29; 7:1–5,9,14–19; 8:1–5,16,20–23; 9:1–5,8–9,13–19,22; 10:1,12,21; 11:1,2,9; 13:17; 14:2–4,15–18,26; 32:34; Dt. 3:26–28; 10:11; Is. 42:7; 45:13; 49:5,6,8,9; 61:1; Mal. 2:6; Mt. 10:8; 28:19,20; Mk. 16:16; Lk. 4:18,19; 7:13,14; Jn. 4:50; 5:6,8; 11:43,44; 21:15,16,17.
    18 Ex. 33:1,3; Num. 33:53; Dt. 1:8; 2:24,31; 4:1; 8:1; 9:23; 11:29,31; Jos. 1:2; Jg. 1:2; Is. 49:8; 58:12; Mt. 17:11; Mk. 9:12.
    19 Mt. 10:8; Lk. 22:35,36.
    20 Mt. 9:37,38; Lk. 10:2; Jn. 4:35–38; 9:4.
    21 Ex. 3:12.

What to say

    22 Ex. 7:2; Jer. 26:2.
    23 Ex. 3:12,14–18; 2 Kg. 22:15–20; 2 Chr. 11:2–4; 20:15; 34:23–28; Is. 22:14; 48:16; Jer. 7:2; 11:2; 17:19,20; 19:1–3; 21:8,11,12; 22:1,2; 26:4; 34:13; 39:16; 42:21; 43:10; 44:24; Ezek. 2:3,4; 3:11,27; 20:3,27,45–47; 21:2,9; 22:3; 24:21; 33:27; 36:1; Zech. 1:3; 2:8,9,11; 4:9; Mal. 4:5; Mt. 15:24; Mk. 9:37; Lk. 4:43; 9:48; 10:16; Jn. 3:17; 4:34; 5:23,24,30,36,37,38; 6:29,38,39,44,46,57; 7:16,28,29,33; 8:16,18,26,28,29,38,40,42; 9:4; 10:36; 12:49,50; 14:10,24; 15:15,21; 16:5,27; 17:3,8,14,18,21,23,25; 20:21.

24 Is. 12:4; 43:21; 61:3; 66:19; Mk. 5:19; Lk. 8:39; Jn. 3:11; 8:49,50,54; 12:27,28; 17:4,6,26.

25 Is. 13:2; 58:1; 61:2; Jer. 4:16; 5:18,19; 13:12,13; 16:10–13; Ezek. 20:4; 22:2; 39:23; Jl. 2:1; Mic. 3:8.

26 Dt. 5:31; Is. 61:2; Mt. 5:19; 10:7; 28:20; Lk. 4:19; 9:60; 10:9; 24:47.

27 Lk. 12:14; Jn. 3:17; 5:30,45–47; 8:15,16,26; 9:39; 12:47.

28 Mt. 13:3–9,18–23; Mk. 4:3–9,13–20; Lk. 8:5–8,10–15.

Some people will accept you

29 Jn. 6:44,45,65; 8:47; 12:44,45; 17:8; 18:37.

30 Is. 52:7; Nah. 1:15; Mt. 11:14.

31 Jer. 2:13; 17:13; Jn. 4:10; 5:21,25,26; 6:32,33,35,48–51,57,58,63; 14:6,19; 15:1.

32 Mt. 13:31,32; Mk. 4:30–32; Lk. 13:18,19.

33 Mt. 13:33; Mk. 4:26–29; Lk. 13:20,21.

34 Num. 6:23–27; Jn. 6:37,39; 10:29; 17:2,6,9,11,12,19,20,24,25.

35 Mt. 9:16,17; 12:30; Mk. 2:21,22; 9:39,40; Lk. 5:36–39; 9:50; 11:23.

Others will reject you

36 Is. 30:9; Jer. 6:17; 26:5; 29:19; Ezek. 2:3,4,6,7; 3:9,26,27; 12:2,3,9; 17:12; 24:3; 44:6; Hos. 10:10; Lk. 22:67, 68; 24:25; Jn 3:11,12,18; 6:36,64; 8:45,46; 10:25,26.

37 Mt. 11:16–19; Lk. 7:31–35.

38 Mt. 12:39–42; 16:4; Mk. 8:12; Lk. 11:29,30; 16:19–31; Jn. 4:48; 6:26.

39 Ezek. 3:4–9; 33:30–32; Zech. 11:7–14; Jn. 5:43.

40 Jer. 7:27–29; Jn. 5:38.

41 Mt. 19:30; 20:1–16; Mk. 10:31; Lk. 13:30.

VI HOW TO COPE WITH TROUBLE

Don't give in to temptation

1 Is. 50:5; Ezek. 14:11; 37:23; Mt. 24:4; Mk. 13:5; Lk. 9:62; 21:8.

2 Ex. 23:2; Dt. 23:9; Is. 33:15; Zech. 3:1,2; Mt. 16:23; Mk. 8:33.

3 Mt. 10:37; 19:29; Mk. 10:29; Lk. 14:26,33; 18:29.

4 Mt. 5:29,30; 16:24; 18:8,9; Mk. 8:34; 9:43–47; Lk. 9:23.

5 Ex. 23:33; 34:12; Num. 33:55,56; Dt. 7:16; 11:16; 12:30; Ezek. 5:7; 11:12.

Bible references (155)

6 Ex. 23:32; 34:12,15,16; Dt. 7:2,3,4; 20:18; Jg. 2:2; 2 Chr. 16:7; Is. 2:6; 30:1; Jer. 15:19; 17:5; Hos 7:8.

7 Ex. 23:24; Lev. 18:3,29,30; 20:23; Dt. 6:14; 7:16; 12:30,31; 18:9; 29:17,18; Jg. 6:10; Jer. 10:2; Ezek. 20:18,32.

8 Dt. 7:25,26.

9 Ex. 34:15:Dt. 13:6–18; 17:2–7.

10 Dt. 6:10–12; 8:11–18; 31:20; Hos.13:6.

11 2 Kg. 21:11; 2 Chr. 21:13; Hos. 4:15; Mt. 18:5,6,7; Mk. 9:42; Lk. 17:1,2; 22:22.

Don't let false prophets influence you

12 Dt. 18:20; Jer. 14:14,15; 23:21, 32; 27, 15; 29:9,31; Ezek. 13:6,7; Mt. 7:15.

13 1 Kg. 22:19–23; 2 Chr. 18:18–22; Jer. 14:14; 23:16,25; 27:10,14,15,16; 29:9,21,23; Ezek. 13:2,3,6,7,8,9; 14:6–10.

14 Mal. 1:6; 2:7.

15 Jer.23:10,18; Ezek. 44:10; Hos. 4:10.

16 Dt. 13:5; Jer. 23:26, 27; 28:16; 29:32; Ezek. 44:12; Zeph. 3:4; Mal. 2:8,9.

17 Jer. 8:8; 29:31.

18 Hos. 4:6.

19 Is. 56:10; Mt. 15:14; Lk. 6:39.

20 Jer. 6:14; 8:11; 14:13,15; 23:16,17; 27:9,14,16; Ezek. 13:6,10,16.

21 Ezek. 13:4; Hos. 6:9; Mt. 7:15.

22 Is. 56:11; Jer. 14:18; 29:23; Hos. 4:8; Mic. 3:11.

23 Is. 28:7,8; Mic. 3:5.

24 Jer. 23:22; 27:18; Ezek. 13:5; Hos. 4:7.

25 Dt. 13:1–3; Is. 9:16; Jer. 23:13,16; 27:9,14,16,17; 29:8; Ezek. 13:10; Mic. 3:5; Mt. 15:14; 24:11.

26 Is. 1:19; Mt. 16:24; Mk. 8:34; Lk. 9:23; 14:26; Jn. 7:17; 12:26; 14:15.

27 Dt. 18:21,22.

28 Mt. 12:33–35; 7:16–20; Lk. 6:43–45.

29 Jn. 7:18.

30 Dt. 13:3.

31 Ex. 22:18; Lev. 19:26,31; 20:6, 27; Dt. 18:10–12,14.

32 Mt. 24:5,23–26; Mk. 13:6,21–23; Lk. 21:8; 17:23.

33 Dt. 13:5; 18:20; Jer. 23:28,33–38; 28:15; Ezek. 12:24; 13:9; 44:13.

34 Jer. 23:28.

Don't turn away from me if you're persecuted

35 Lev. 20:24,26; Jn. 8:23; 15:19; 17:11,14,16,25; 18:36.

36 Mt. 10:22; 24:9; Mk. 13:13; Lk. 21:17; Jn. 7:7; 15:18,19,24,25; 17:14.

37 Mt. 10:24,25; Lk. 6:40; Jn. 13:15,16; 15:20,24.

38 Is. 49:7; 53:3,4; Mt. 21:42; Mk. 12:10; Lk. 20:17; Jn. 8:49.

39 Mt. 10:16,34; Lk. 10:3, 12:49,51.

40 Mt. 10:21,35; Mk. 13:12; Lk. 12:52,53.

41 Jer. 12:6; Mt. 10:36; 13:57; Mk. 6:4; Lk. 4:23–27; 21:16.

42 Zech. 13:7; Mt. 26:31,32,34; Mk. 14:27,28,30,41; Lk. 22:21,34,48,52,53; Jn. 13:21,26,27,38; 16:32.

43 Mt. 10:25; 12:25–29; Mk. 3:23–27; Lk. 11:17–23; Jn. 8:49; 10:34–38.

44 Is. 52:14; 53:3,8,12; Mt. 10:17,18,19; 17:11,12; 27:46; Mk. 13:9,11;·14:34,41,42; 15:34; Lk. 12:11; 21:12,13; 22:15,37; Jn. 10:32; 15:21; 16:2; 18:23; 19:28,30.

45 Is. 53:8,9; Mt. 24:9; Lk. 11:49; 21:16; Jn. 16:2–4.

46 Mt. 5:10; Mk. 10:30; Jn. 15:20.

47 Mt. 5:17; 17:22; 20:18,19; 26:2,21,23,24,38,39,45,46,52–56; Mk. 9:12,13,31; 10:33,34; Mk. 14:18,20,21,48,49; Lk. 4:21; 9:22,44; 17:25; 18:31–33; 22:22,37; 24:25,26,44,46; Jn. 5:39; 13:18,19.

48 1 Sam 9:16; Is. 53:4–6,8,10–12; Mt. 20:28; 26:28; Mk. 10:45; Lk. 19:10; Jn. 1:29, 36; 5:34; 11:49,50; 12:47.

49 Is. 53:12; Zech. 9:11; Mt. 26:26–28; Mk. 14:22,24; Lk. 22:17,19,20; Jn. 6:51; 10:18; 12:24; 15:13.

50 Mt. 10:39; 16:25,26; Mk. 8:35,36,37; Lk. 9:24,25; 17:33; Jn. 10:15,17; 12:25.

51 Ezek. 2:8; Mt. 16:24; 20:22,23; 26:42; Mk. 8:34; 10:38–40; Lk. 9:23; 12:50; 14:27; 22:42; Jn. 18:11.

52 Jl. 3:2; Zech. 1:21; Mt. 8:20; 10:23; Lk. 9:58; Jn. 16:33.

53 Jer. 29:4–9.

54 Is. 10:24; 51:7,8,13; Jer. 42:11; Ezek. 2:6; Jn. 19:11.

55 Is. 50:6; 53:7; Lk. 23:34.

56 Mt. 5:11,12; Lk. 6:22,23,26.

Keep watch over yourself!

57 Mt. 24:10,12; Lk. 18:8.

58 Mt. 10:22; 24:13; Mk. 13:13; Lk. 21:19; 22:28; Jn. 16:1.

59 Dt. 4:9; Lk. 11:35.

60 Num. 15:38,39; Dt. 6:4–9; 11:18–21; 22:12; Jos. 1:8; Ezek. 40:4; Mal. 3:16.

Bible references (157)

61 Is. 51:2; Jer. 6:16; 31:21; Mic. 6:5; Mt. 13:51,52; Jn. 5:41,44.

62 Mt. 26:41; Mk. 14:38; Lk. 21:36; 22:40,46; Jn. 17:15.

63 Mt. 24:28,36; 25:13; Mk. 13:32; Lk. 12:40; 17:37; 21:34,35.

64 Mt. 24:42–44; Lk. 21:34.

65 Lk. 12:35–39.

66 Mt. 24:45–51; Mk. 13:33–37; Lk. 12:42–48.

67 Mt. 25:1–13.

68 Dt. 11:28; 27:15–26; 28:15,45; 29:20,21,27; Jer. 11:3, 8; 17:5; 48:10; Mal. 3:9.

VII WHAT HAPPENS IF YOU BREAK MY AGREEMENT?

Your thinking gets twisted

1 Jn. 3:20,21; 11:9.

2 Is. 29:13; 48:1,2; 58:2; Jer. 3:5; 7:9,10; 44:26; Hos. 8:2; 10:2; Mt. 15:7,8; Mk. 7:6; Lk. 16:15; Jn. 8:54,55.

3 Mt. 7:21; 21:28–31; Lk. 6:46; Jn. 14:21,23.

4 Dt. 29:19; Jer. 3:4,5; 21:13; Am. 9:10; Mic. 3:11.

5 Mt. 3:9; Lk. 3:8.

6 Am. 5:18; Zeph. 1:14.

7 Is. 19:13; Jer. 7:8; 10:3; 13:25; Ezek. 21:29; Am. 2:4; Mt. 15:3–6,9; Mk. 7:7–13.

8 Dt. 31:17; 1 Sam. 15:22; Is. 1:11–14; 58:3–6; Jer. 6:20; 7:21; 11:15; 50:7; Hos. 6:6; 8:13; Am. 4:4,5; 5:21–23,25; Zech. 7:5–7; Mal. 2:13,14; Mt. 12:7; 9:13.

9 Mt. 15:10,11,17–20; Mk. 7:15, 18–23.

10 Jer. 7:4; Am. 2:8; Mt. 15:9; 24:15; Mk. 7:7; 13:14.

11 Num. 14:27; Is. 29:15,16; 45:9–11; Jer. 2:29; 5:14; Ezek. 18:29; 33:17–20.

12 Num. 14:20–25; 15:30; 2 Kg. 19:22–24,27,28; Is. 5:18,19; 37:28,29.

13 Is. 40:27; 47:10; 49:14; Jer. 5:12,13; 6:10; Ezek. 8:12; 9:9; Zeph. 1:12.

14 Mal. 2:17; 3:13–15.

15 Is. 5:20; Jer. 2:35; 3:21; 23:36; Hos. 9:7.

16 Is. 17:10; 45:4,5; 51:13; Jer. 3:21; 4:22; 9:3,6; 13:25; 18:15; Ezek. 22:12; Hos. 4:1; 5:4; 8:14; 13:6; Mic. 4:12; Jn. 7:28; 8:14,19,55; 15:21.

17 Ex. 20:5; Num. 14:11,23; 15:31; Dt. 5:9; 7:10; 2 Sam. 12:9; Is. 1:4; 5:24; 29:20; 30:12; 43:22; 45:24; 52:5; Jer. 6:10; Ezek. 22:8; Hos. 8:12.

18 Lev. 22:9; Jer. 12:8; 34:16; Ezek. 20:17; 39:23; 43:8; Hos. 4:2; Nah. 1:9,11; Mt. 11:12; Lk. 16:16.

19 Jer. 7:19; Mt. 6:22,23; Lk. 11:34,36; Jn. 6:53.

20 Gen 4:7; Jos. 24:19; 1 Kg. 21:20; Jer. 2:14; 4:22; 13:23; 17:9; Am. 3:10; Mt. 12:34; Jn. 3:19; 8:34,35,44.

I reject you

21 Dt. 29:20; Jos. 24:19; Is. 22:14; 42:24; Jer. 5:7; 50:7; Ezek. 24:13; Hos. 1:6; 6:11–7:1; Mt. 6:15.

22 Ex. 23:7; Num. 14:34; Dt. 7:10; Is. 7:13; 43:24; 47:3; 51:20; 65:6; Jer. 4:28; 6:11; 13:14; 15:6; Ezek. 5:11; 7:4,9; 8:18; 9:10; 24:14; Hos. 1:6; Jl. 3:21; Am. 1:3,6,9,11, 13; 2:1, 4,6; 4:12; Nah. 1:3; Zech. 8:14; 11:6.

23 Lev. 7:18; 26:31; Is. 9:17; 27:11; Jer. 14:10,12; 16:5,13; 19:7; 49:20; 50:45; Hos. 1:9; 9:15; 13:14; Mt. 10:38; Lk. 14:26,27,33; Jn. 5:37,38; 5:42; 8:46,47.

24 Dt. 31:17,18; Is. 1:15; 54:7,8; 57:17; 59:2; Jer. 11:11,14; 14:12; 18:17; 33:5; Ezek. 7:22; 8:18; 39:23,24; Hos. 5:6; Jl. 1:19; Mic. 3:4.

25 Ex. 32:33; Lev. 26:30; Num. 14:12; Dt. 23:14; 31:17; Jos. 7:12; 1 Sam. 15:23; 2 Kg. 21:14; 23:27; 2 Chr. 12:5; 15:2; 24:20; Is. 2:6; 7:9; 29:2; 54:7; 59:15; Jer. 6:8,30; 7:29; 11:15; 12:7,8; 17:4; Hos. 5:6; 9:12,15; Am. 5:2; 9:7; Nah. 3:6; Zech. 8:17; Mal. 1:3; Mt. 23:38; Lk. 13:35; Jn. 13:8.

26 2 Kg. 19:28; Is. 37:29; Jer. 8:13; Ezek. 38:4.

27 Dt. 29:18; Is. 5:1–7; Jer. 2:21; 5:10; 8:13; 24:8; 29:17; Ezek. 5:11; Hos. 9:16; Mt. 15:13; Lk. 13:6–9; Jn. 15:2.

28 Is. 1:21; 50:1; Jer. 2:2,23–25,36; 3:1–3,11,14,20; 4:30; 5:11; 30:14; 31:22,32; Ezek. 5:5–7; 15:8; 16:2–52, 56,57; 23:2–49; Hos. 1:2; 2:2–9;3:1; 5:3,4,7; 6:4,7,10; 9:1; Mt. 17:17; Mk. 9:19; Lk. 9:41.

29 Jos. 24:20; Is. 22:8.

30 Lev. 17:10; 20:6; 26:17,41; Dt. 11:2; 2 Kg. 22:19; 2 Chr. 34:27; Is. 5:25; 14:22; 28:21; 31:2; Jer. 6:12; 18:17; 21:10,13; 44:11; Ezek. 5:8; 14:8; 15:7; 21:3,17; 25:6,13,16; 26:3; 28:21,22; 35:2,3; Hos. 10:10; Am. 1:8; 3:1; Nah. 2:13; 3:5; Zeph. 1:4; 2:5,13; Zech. 9:1.

31 Ex. 22:24; Dt. 11:17; 29:20,28; 2 Kg. 22:17; 2 Chr. 19:2; 28:11; 34:25; Is. 1:24; 9:19; 13:13; 42:25; 51:20; 59:18; 60:10; 63:4,5; 66:15; Jer. 4:4,26; 5:29; 6:11; 7:29; 15:14; 17:4; 21:5,12; 23:20; 33:5; 42:18; 44:6; Ezek. 5:13,15; 6:12; 7:3,8,12,13,14; 8:18; 21:17,31; 22:31; 30:15; 36:18; Mic. 5:15; Nah. 1:2; Zeph. 1:15; 2:2; 3:8; Zech. 7:12.

32 2 Kg. 21:14; 23:27; Is. 22:19; Jer. 7:15; 9:15; 25:38; 32:31; Ezek. 16:50; Hos. 5:12,15; 9:17; Mic. 5:3.

You get confused and distressed

33 Is. 53:6; 57:17; 65:2; 66:3; Jer. 7:24; 8:6; 9:14,26; 10:23; 11:8; 13:10; 16:12.

34 Is. 1:3; Jer. 8:7.

35 Hos. 5:11; 13:13.

36 Is. 5:21; 47:10; 50:11.

37 Ex. 32:9; 33:3,5; Dt. 9:6,13; 31:27; 1 Sam. 15:23; 2 Chr. 16:9; Is. 5:13; 46:12; 48:4,8; 59:8; Jer. 4:22; 5:3,23; 6:10,28; 7:26; 10:14; 17:23; 18:15; 19:15; Hos. 4:16; 7:9; Zech. 7:11,12; Lk. 24:25; Jn. 8:43.

38 Jer. 7:24; 8:4; 15:6.

39 2 Chr. 18:16; Is. 53:6; Jer. 14:10; 50:6; Ezek. 34:5,6; Zech. 10:2.

40 Dt. 28:28,29; Is. 27:11; 50:10; 59:9,10; Jer. 4:22; Hos. 4:14; Zeph. 1:17; Mt. 8:10–12; 15:16; 25:30; Mk. 7:18; Jn. 11:10; 12:35.

41 Is. 8:14,15; 28:13; Jer. 6:21; Hos. 14:9; Lk. 20:18.

42 Is. 3:8; 59:10; Jer. 5:21; 18:15; Hos. 5:5; 14:1; Jn. 9:41; 11:10.

43 Dt. 28:65; Is. 5:30; 23:12; 29:2; 48:22; 57:20,21; 59:8; Jer. 10:18; 16:5; Ezek. 7:25; 22:5; Mic. 1:12; Zeph. 1:15.

44 Lev. 26:16,17,36,37; Dt. 28:67; Is. 42:22; 44:11; 50:11; Jer. 49:5; 50:17; Am. 5:19,20.

45 Is. 1:4; 13:6; 29:2; 59:11; 65:14; Hos. 7:14; Jl. 1:8; Mic. 2:4; Mt. 8:12; 13:42,50; 24:51; 25:30; Lk. 6:25; 13:28.

46 Lev. 26:21; Dt. 28:27,35,66; Is. 1:5,6; Jer. 46:11.

47 Lev. 26:16,39; Dt. 28:65; Is. 59:10; Ezek. 4:17; 24:22,23; 33:10.

48 Is. 1:30; Jer. 17:6; Hos. 2:3; 13:15.

You're good for nothing

49 Dt. 28:20; Is. 3:11; 19:3; 45:16; Jer. 17:6.

50 Is. 55:2; Hag. 1:9.

51 Dt. 28:16,17,19,20,48; Is. 65:13; Jer. 12:13; Mic. 6:14; Hag. 1:5,6.

52 Lev. 26:22; Dt. 28:18,32; Hos. 9:11,12,16.

53 Lev. 26:22; Dt. 4:27; 28:62; Hos. 13:3; Nah. 1:14.

54 Dt. 28:29,63; 2 Chr. 24:20; Is. 47:11; Jer. 4:13; Ezek. 18:30; Hos. 4:14; Mic. 2:4; Hab. 2:4.

55 Dt. 28:43,44; Is. 17:4; Jer. 49:15; Ezek. 24:25; Ob. 2.

56 Dt. 28:29; Is. 51:19; Jer. 2:36,37; 15:5; 30:13; Hos. 5:14; Am. 5:2.

57 Is. 22:18; 44:9,11; 45:16; 65:13; Jer. 13:22,26; 14:3; 15:9; 17:13.

58 Num. 11:20; Dt. 28:25,37,46; 1 Kg. 9:7; 2 Chr. 7:20–22; Is. 43:28; 65:15; Jer. 13:10,22; 15:4; 18:16; 19:8; 22:8,9; 24:9; 26:6; 29:18; 34:17; 42:18; 44:8,12; Ezek. 5:14,15; 14:8; 22:4,5; Hos. 7:16; 8:8; Mic. 2:4; 6:16; Zech. 8:13; Mt. 25:30.

There's no hope for you

59 Jer. 31:20; Hos. 11:8,9.

60 Is. 43:27; 54:6; 65:1,2,3,12; Jer. 7:13,26; 22:21; 32:33; 34:14; 35:17; Hos. 11:2; Zeph. 3:7; Hag. 2:17; Zech. 1:2; 7:13.

61 Is. 42:25; Jer. 12:11; Hos. 11:3.

62 Lev. 26:18,23,24,27; Is. 40:2; Jer. 2:30; 5:3; 16:18; Hos. 10:10.

63 Jer. 6:28–30; Ezek. 22:18–22; 24:6–14.

64 Is. 5:25; 9:12,17,21; 10:4; 28:19; 46:12; 59:11; Jer. 4:8; Ezek. 7:4,9; 13:9; 20:38; 24:24; 25:5,7,11; 26:6; 28:22; 29:6,9,16; 30:19,25,26; 32:15; 35:4,9.

65 Mt. 12:31,32; Mk. 3:28,29; Lk. 12:10.

66 Dt. 29:4; Is. 6:9,10; 44:18; Hos. 5:4; Lk. 19:42.

67 Jer. 17:1.

68 Is. 30:12–14.

69 Is. 28:20; Jer. 14:17; 30:12,13,15; Mic. 1:9; Nah. 3:19.

70 Jer. 7:16; 11:14; 14:11; 15:1,2; Am. 7:8; 8:2; Mal. 1:4.

71 Is. 34:2,5; Jer. 4:18; Ezek. 30:9; Jn. 6:67,70; 8:38; 17:12.

72 Is. 7:17; 10:3; 13:6,9; 31:2; 47:11; Jer. 11:11; 46:21; Ezek. 5:9; 7:2,3,6,7,10; 21:25,29; 22:14; 30:2,3; Jl. 1:15; 2:1,11; 3:14; Nah. 1:6; 3:6; Zeph. 1:7,14; 2:11; Zech. 14:1; Mal. 3:2; 4:5.

73 Is. 28:21; Jer. 46:10; Ezek. 26:21; 27:36; Jn. 7:33,34; 8:21; 13:33.

74 Is. 27:11; Ezek. 15:2–6; Jn. 15:6.

75 Ex. 32:10; 33:5; Num. 16:21,24,45; Dt. 4:24; 28:21; Jos. 24:20; Is. 1:28,31; 33:11,12,14; 42:25; 66:15; Jer. 11:16; 21:10,14; 22:7; 27:8; Ezek. 15:7; 20:47,48; 22:31; 30:8,14,16; 43:8; Am. 4:11; 5:6,7; Ob. 18; Nah. 1:10; 3:13,15; Mal. 4:1; Mt. 7:19; 13:42,50; 25:41.

76 2 Kg. 21:12; Jer. 19:3; Ezek. 5:8; 39:21.

77 Ex. 17:14; 28:35,43; 30:20,21; Lev. 16:2,13; 22:9; 23:30; 26:38; Num. 4:20; 18:3; 26:65; Dt. 4:26; 6:15; 7:4; 8:19,20; 9:8,14; 11:17; 28:20,45,51,61,63; 29:20; 30:18; Jos. 7:12; 2 Kg. 1:3,4.16; 2 Chr. 25:16; Is. 14:20; 22:4,18; 65:15; 66:17; Jer. 5:10; 6:2; 12:17; 15:6,7; 17:13; 22:12,26; 25:9; 27:10; 42:16; 48:35; Ezek. 5:16; 25:7,16; 26:21; Hos. 8:4; 13:9; Am. 8:2; 9:8; Nah. 1:14; Lk. 13:3,5; Jn. 8:21,24; Mt. 5:29,30; 18:8,9; 25:46; Mk. 9:43,45,47.

Bible references (161)

VIII WHAT HELL ON EARTH WOULD BE LIKE

People reject me

1 Dt. 8:19; 11:28; 30:17; 31:16; Jos. 24:20; Jg. 10:13; Is. 57:5; Jer. 2:20; Ezek. 14:3; 16:43; 20:8,39; 22:9; Hos. 4:12; 7:4.

2 Ex. 32:8; Dt. 17:3; 29:26; 31:18; 1 Sam. 8:8; 1 Kg. 9:6,9; 11:33; 2 Chr. 7:19,22; 25:15; Is. 57:6,9; 65:3,5,11; 66:17; Jer. 2:23; 3:13; 5:19; 7:9,17,18; 8:2,19; 9:14; 11:10,17; 13:10,27; 16:11,13,18; 17:2,3; 18:15; 22:9; 32:29; 44:3,8,25; Ezek. 8:9,12,17; 11:21; 14:7; 18:11,12; 20:16,24,27-31; 22:9; 33:25; 43:8; Hos. 4:13; 7:14,16; 9:15; 11:2.

3 Is. 57:7,8; Jer. 7:31; 19:4,5; 32:35; Hos. 9:1.

4 Jer. 50:38; Hos 10:1.

5 Dt. 4:18; 9:12; 28:36,64; 1 Kg. 14:9; 2 Kg. 1:16; 2 Chr. 25:15; Is. 2:8; 16:12; 28:15; 43:8,9; 44:9-11; 48:14; Jer. 2:10,11; 5:7; Ezek. 22:4; Hos. 4:12; 8:4; 13:1,2; Am. 5:26; 8:14.

6 Is. 66:3; Jer. 2:11; 49:16, Ezek. 22:3; 36:18; Hos. 8:11; Mic. 6:16; Hab. 2:13.

7 Is. 45:20; Jer. 3:6-10; 44:5; Hos. 9:10.

8 2 Kg. 1:3; 22:17; 2 Chr. 34:25; Is. 57:6; 65:7.

9 Is. 2:6; 19:3; 65:4; Zech. 10:2.

10 Is. 43:27; Jer. 6:13; 23:11-14; Ezek. 7:26; Hos. 9:7-9.

11 Is. 29:9-12; 42:18-20.

12 Is. 30:10,11; Jer. 5:30,31; Mic 2:6,11.

13 Is. 44:25; Jer. 8:9; 23:10,15; 49:7; Ob. 8; Zech. 5:5-11.

People mistreat my followers

14 Num. 14:22; Dt. 8:20; 28:45,62; Jg. 2:20; 6:10; 1 Kg. 9:6; 2; Chr. 16:7; 25:16; Is. 8:6; 9:13; 28:12; 30:9; 43:22; 50:2; 57:10; 59:13; Jer. 3:13; 5:3,24; 6:15; 7:24,26; 8:5,6,12; 9:5,13; 11:8; 12:17; 13:10,11; 15:7; 16:12; 17:23,27; 19:15; 22:5,21; 25:7,8; 26:4; 27:8; 34:17; 35:13-16; 36:31; 42:13,21; 44:5,10; 50:14; Hos. 7:10,14; 9:17; 11:5; Am. 4:6,8-11; Zeph. 1:6; 3:2; Zech. 14:17,18; Mal. 2:2; Mt. 10:38; Lk. 14:27; Jn. 5:40; 8:37; 12:47,48; 14:24.

15 Jer. 5:4,5.

16 Is. 28:9,10; Mt. 23:37; Lk. 13:34.

17 2 Chr. 19:2; Is. 59:15; Ezek. 35:5; Am. 1:9; 2:12; Mic. 1:13.

18 Is. 57:3,4; Jer. 50:11; Ezek. 21:28; 25:3,6,8,12,15; 29:6,7; Jl. 3:3-6; Am. 1:3,6; 2:6; 5:12; Ob. 10-14; Zeph. 2:8,10; Lk. 11:31,32.

19 Is. 9:17; 57:1,2; Jer. 2:30; Mic. 7:1,2; Mt. 23:37; Lk. 5:34,35; 13:34; Jn. 8:37,39-41; 14:19; 16:20.

20 Am. 8:11,12; Mt. 23:39; Lk. 13:35; 17:22.

(162)   "Hello I'm God & I'm here to help you"

21 Mt. 21:33–40; Mk. 12:1–9; Lk. 20:9–16.
22 Is. 42:13; Jer. 25:30–32; Jer. 45:5; Ezek. 21:26; Jl. 3:16; Am. 1:2; 5:17; Ob. 15; Mic. 1:3.
23 Is. 31:2; Ezek. 12:22,23,25,27,28; 22:14; Hos. 10:15; Am. 4:12; Hab. 1:5.

People aren't ashamed when they do wrong

24 Is. 3:9; 5:18; 59:3,9,14; 66:3; Jer. 30:14,15; Ezek. 21:24; Hos. 13:12; Am. 5:7; Zeph. 2:1.
25 Is. 29:20; 59:6,7; Jer. 5:6,28; 9:3; Ezek. 8:13; Jl. 3:13; Mic. 7:3.
26 Is. 59:5,6; Jer. 6:7; Mic. 2:1.
27 Is. 1:21,23; 3:9; 5:23; 10:1,2; 29:21; 33:8; 59:4,8,9,11,14,15; Jer. 5:2,28; 7:9; Ezek. 7:10; 9:9; Hos. 10:13; Am. 5:7,10,12; 6:12; Mic. 7:3; Zeph. 3:3,5; Zech. 5:2–4; Mal. 3:5.
28 Is. 2:7; 5:8,14; 16:6; 32:9; 37:23–25; Jer. 5:27; 17:11; 22:13,14; 48:29,30; Ezek. 7:10; 16:49,50; Hab. 2:6–8; Zeph. 1:12; Zech. 11:5; Mal. 4:1.
29 Is. 5:11,12,22; Hos. 4:11; Am. 4:1; Hab. 2:5.
30 Is. 1:23; 3:5; 5:7; 30:12; 59:13; Jer. 5:26,28; 6:6; 9:6; 22:13; Ezek. 16:49; 18:12; 22:7,29; Ezek. 34:21; Hos. 12:7; Am. 1:11; 2:7; 4:1; 5:11; Zeph. 3:1; Mal. 3:5; Mt. 17:17; 25:42–45; Lk. 9:41.
31 Dt. 15:11; Jos. 7:11; Is. 9:19; 10:2; 24:16; 33:8; 42:22; 48:8; 57:17; Jer. 5:27; 6:13; 7:9; 8:5,10; 9:2,5,6,8; 22:17; Ezek. 18:10,12,13,18; 22:7,12,13,29; Hos. 4:2; 7:1,16; 11:12; 12:7; Am. 4:1; 5:11; 8:4–6; Mic. 2:2; 6:10–12; 7:4,5; Hab. 2:5,9,11; Zeph. 1:9; Zech. 5:3,4.
32 Jos. 7:11; Is. 5:18; 9:17; 33:8; 59:3,13–15; Jer. 6:28; 8:6; 9:3–5; Ezek. 16:59; Hos. 4:1,2; 10:4,13; 12:1; Mal. 2:10; Jn. 8:44,55.
33 2 Sam. 12:11,12; Jer. 5:7,8; 7:9; 9:2; Ezek. 18:11; 22:10,11; 33:26; Hos. 4:2,13,14; Am. 2:7; Mal. 3:5.
34 Is. 65:4; 66:17; Ezek. 4:13; 22:10; 33:25; Hos. 9:3,4.
35 Gen. 8:21; Is. 1:4; 3:5; 57:5; Ezek. 22:7; Hos. 5:7; Jl. 3:3; Mic. 7:6; Jn. 21:18.
36 Gen. 9:5,6; Is. 1:15,21; 5:7; 59:3,6,7; Jer. 2:34; 6:7; 7:9; 13:22; 22:17; Ezek. 7:11,23; 8:17; 9:9; 11:6; 12:19; 18:10; 22:3,4,9,12,13; 24:6–9; 33:25,26; 36:18; Hos. 4:2; 6:8; 7:4–7; 12:1; Jl. 3:19; Am. 1:11; 3:10; Mic. 6:12; 7:2; Hab. 2:12,15–17; Zeph. 1:9; Zech. 8:10; 11:5.
37 Is. 9:18; Mal. 1:4; Mt. 24:36–38; Lk. 17:26–28.

People choose bad leaders

38 Is. 28:14; 51:18; Hos. 8:4; 9:15.
39 Is. 3:4,12; 56:11,12; Hos. 7:5.
40 Is. 3:12, 5:13; Jer. 8:9; Mic. 3:9–11.
41 Lev. 4:22–26; 1 Kg. 16:1–4; Ezek. 21:25; Hos. 5:1,2; 7:3.
42 Is. 1:23; 3:13–15; Zech. 11:6.
43 Jer. 10:21; 13:20; 23:1; 50:6; Ezek. 34:2–4,7,8,18,19; Nah. 3:18; Zech. 11:5.
44 Ezek. 22:6,25,27; Mic. 3:1–3; Zeph. 3:3.
45 Hos. 7:7; 13:9–11.
46 Is. 22:8–11; 30:15,16; Hos. 10:13,14; Jl. 3:9,10; Mt. 24:6; Mk. 13:7.
47 2 Chr. 20:37; Is. 19:11–15; 20:1–6; 28:14,15; 28:18; 30:1–7; 31:1,3; 57:9; Jer. 2:18,33,37; 13:21; 46:25; Ezek. 30:6; Hos. 5:13; 7:11; 8:9,10; 12:1; Ob. 7; Nah. 3:8,9; Zeph. 1:8.

Nations war against each other

48 2 Chr. 15:6; 16:9; Mt. 24:7; Mk. 13:8; Lk. 21:10.
49 Is. 5:26; 9:11; 19:1; 21:5; Jer. 4:6; 5:15; 6:1,22; 13:20; 33:5; 46:18; 48:11; 49:31; 50:3,9,25; Ezek. 7:24; Am. 6:14; Ob. 1; Mic. 1:9,15; Zeph. 1:10.
50 Jer. 8:16; 12:12; 15:8; 22:7; 48:15; 50:22.
51 Is. 2:10,19,21; Jer. 4:5,29; 6:1; 46:22; 48:6,28.
52 Dt. 28:49; Is. 5:26; Jer. 16:16; 48:16,40; 49:22; 50:29; Hos. 8:1,3.
53 Dt. 28:49,50; Is. 5:26–30; 13:9; 28:2,17; 66:15; Jer. 4:7,13; 5:15,16; 6:23; 21:7; 23:19; 30:23,24; 46:22,23; 49:19; 50:9,41,42; Jl. 1:6; 2:2,11; Hab. 1:5–11.
54 Is. 7:18,19; 29:3; Jer. 4:16,17; 6:3,25; 46:20,23; Ezek. 26:8; Am. 3:11; Mic. 5:1; Lk. 19:43.
55 Dt. 28:52,53,55,57; Is. 29:3; Nah. 3:14; Zech. 12:2.
56 Lev. 26:29; Dt. 28:53–57; Is. 9:20; Jer. 19:9; Ezek. 5:10.
57 Is. 28:18,19; Jer. 6:4,5.
58 Jer. 2:13; Am. 2:15; 5:3; Nah. 3:12.
59 Is. 19:2.
60 Lev. 26:37; Dt. 28:25; Jos. 7:12,13; Jg. 2:3; Is. 10:16; 13:14; 19:1,3; 30:16,17; 42:14; 51:20; Jer. 4:19,31; 6:24,25; 13:21; 22:23; 46:21; 48:41; 49:22–24,37; 50:28; 51:6,8,9,14,30,32; Ezek. 30:24; Nah. 3:13; Zeph. 1:14.
61 Dt. 28:52; Is. 17:3; 25:12; Jer. 5:17; 33:4,5; 48:1,7,41; 49:35;

50:15; 51:32; Ezek. 24:25; 26:4,9,10; 30:16; Hos. 8:14; 10:14; Am. 1:4,5,7,10,12,14; 2:2; 3:11; 4:10; 6:8; Mic. 5:10,11; Nah. 2:13; 3:13; Zeph. 1:16.

62 Lev. 26:25; Dt. 28:25; 2 Kg. 21:14; Is. 22:25; 28:19; 42:24; Jer. 6:15; 8:12; 12:7; 16:16; 20:4; 21:3,4,7,10; 22:24,25; 25:27; 32:28; 34:2–5,20–22; 38:3; 46:15,16,24,26; 47:2,3; 48:1; 50:2,15; Ezek. 30:12; 39:23; Hos. 1:5; 10:9; Am. 5:1,2; 6:8; 8:14; Nah. 2:13; Zeph. 1:3; 3:6; Zech. 14:2.

63 Is. 28:11; Jer. 5:15; Ezek. 11:9.

64 Is. 5:14; 14:9–20; 52:5; Jer. 4:9; 22:22; 23:2; 25:34–38; 49:38; 50:35,43; Ezek. 7:27; 12:9–15; 21:26; 32:18–32; 34:9,10; Hos. 5:10; 7:16; 10:3,7,15; Am. 1:5,8; 2:3; Nah. 3:10,15–17; Zech. 10:3; 11:15–17.

65 Ezek. 7:19–21; Zeph. 1:11.

66 Dt. 28:30; Is. 13:16; 26:20,21; Jer. 6:12; 8:10; Hos. 13:16; Jl. 2:6–9; Am. 1:13; Zech. 14:2; Mo. 24:19; Mk. 13:17; Lk. 21:23.

67 Is. 13:16,18; 19:10; 24:2; Jer. 5:17; 6:11; 13:14; 15:9; 19:7; 20:4; 21:7; 49:10,21; 50:45; Ezek. 5:17; 9:1,6,7; 24:21,25; 26:11; Hos. 10:14; 13:16; Am. 9:4; Nah. 3:10; Lk. 19:44.

68 Is. 15:5 Jer. 48:45; 49:5,8,25,30; 50:8,16; Nah. 3:11; Mt. 3:7; Mk. 13:14; Lk. 3:7.

69 Is. 14:24; 22:1–8; 28:18; Jer. 47:3.

70 Is. 15:7; Mt. 24:15–18,20; Mk. 13:15,16; Lk. 17:31,32; 21:21.

71 Is. 5:29; 24:17,18; Jer. 48:43,44; 50:24; Am. 2:14–16.

72 Lev. 26:17; 2 Kg. 21:14; Is. 5:25,29; 7:20; 8:6–8; 28:17; 42:22; 56:9; 57:17; 60:10; Jer. 2:14; 5:6; 8:17; 33:5; 43:11; 48:9,12,25, 38, 39; 49:16; Ezek. 9:5; 25:9; 26:19; 30:21, 22, 24, 25; Hos. 5:14; 6:1; 7:12; 9:13,16; 13:7,8; Am. 9:2,3; Ob. 4; Mic. 6:13.

73 Is. 10:4; 16:14; 24:22.

74 Dt. 31:17; 2 Chr. 7:13; Is. 1:7; 9:12; 13:16; Jer. 6:9; 8:16; 12:9; 49:9,10; 50:10,17; Ezek. 12:19; Hos. 8:8; Ob. 5,6; Zeph. 1:13; Zech. 2:9; 14:2.

75 Lev. 26:16; Dt. 28:30,31,33,51; Jer. 5:17; 6:12; 48:32; 49:32; Ezek. 7:24; 25:4; Hos. 5:7; Am. 4:9, 5:11; Mic. 6:15; Zeph. 1:13.

76 Jer. 8:10; 15:13; 17:3; 20:5; Ezek. 24:25; 26:5 Jl. 3:2; Mic. 2:4,5; Zech. 14:1.

77 Lev. 26:22; 2 Kg. 21:13; 2 Chr. 20:37; Is. 8:4; 10:16–19,33,34; 13:19; 14:8; 15:5; 16:14; 17:3; 21:1,2; 47:1–3; Jer. 22:7; 47:4,5; 48:3,4,36,42; 49:29; 50:26,37; 51:1,2,54,55,56,58; Ezek. 7:11; 25:7; 26:12; 27:25–27,32–34; 29:18–20; 30:4,10; 35:10–15; Am. 3:15; 4:9; 6:11; Zech. 9:3,4.

78 Lev. 26:41; Dt. 28:36,37,41,48,63,68; 29:28; 2 Chr. 7:20;
Is. 5:13; 6:12; 22:17,18; 27:7,8; 39:5–7; Jer. 5:19; 8:3; 9:16; 10:18;
15:2,14; 16:13; 17:4; 20:4,5; 22:11,12,26; 24:9; 27:10; 29:18,20;
43:11; 45:4; 46:19; 48:46; 50:9,33; Ezek. 30:17,18; 32:9; Hos.
8:10,13; 9:3,6; 10:11; 11:5,7; Am. 1:5,15; 4:2,3; 5:27; 7:17; 9:4; Mic.
1:16; 2:3; 4:10; Nah. 3:10; Zeph. 2:4; Zech. 7:14; 14:2; Lk. 21:24.

79 Lev. 26:33; Dt. 4:27; 28:48,64,68; Is. 52:3–5; Jer. 5:19;
9:16; 13:25; 15:14; 17:4; 18:17; 25:11; 27:5–7,11; 28:13,14; 49:32,36;
Ezek. 5:10,12; 20:23; 22:15; 25:4,10; 29:12; 30:23,26; 36:19; Zeph.
2:2; Zech. 2:6; 7:14; 10:9.

80 Lev. 26:17,38; Num. 14:23; 20:12,24–26; Dt. 1:34–36;
28:29,33; Is. 19:4; 23:12; Jer. 22:12,27; 42:18; 46:16; 50:33; Ezek.
20:38; Hos. 5:11; 9:3; 11:5; Am. 2:13; 6:14; Zech. 9:12.

81 2 Kg. 22:19; Is. 3:26; Jer. 25:9; 46:12,24; 48:1,39;
49:13,17,18; 51:47; Nah. 3:5,6,7; Ob. 10; Zeph. 2:15.

82 Dt. 29:22–24; 1 Kg. 9:8,9; Jer. 32:32.

83 Is. 34:12; Jer. 48:2; Ezek. 21:32; 25:7,10; 26:21; 27:36;
Hos. 1:4; Nah. 2:13.

Powerful nations rise and fall

84 Is. 13:3,4,17,22; 14:29–31; 18:1,2; 33:1,7; 41:2–4,25; 45:1–
3; 46:11; 48:14,15; Jer. 25:8,9,12,14; 49:19,28,30; 50:9,14,15,21;
51:7,11,12,20–23,27,28,33,49; Ezek. 26:3,7; 30:11,24,25; Hos.
10:10; Am. 6:13.

85 Is. 21:11,12; 40:23,24.

86 2 Kg. 19:25,26; Is. 9:8–10; 10:5–15; 14:5,6; 21:9; 23:9,12;
25:11; 28:1,3,4; 37:26,27; 47:5–7; Jer. 46:3–12; 48:14,18–
20,26,27,42,45; 49:4; 50:11,12,23,29,31,32,44; 51:8,11–13,30–
32,38–42,44,53,55; Ezek. 7:12,13,24; 27:2–25; 28:2–10; 29:9,10;
30:6,18; 32:12,23–27,30,32; 33:28; Am. 6:1–3; Ob. 3; Mic. 1:15;
Zeph. 2:15; Hag. 2:21,22; Zech. 1:15; 9:6; 10:11; Mt. 11:21–24;
Lk. 10:13–15.

87 Ezek. 29:2–5; 32:2–7.

88 Ezek. 31:2–18.

89 Is. 13:7,8; 33:14; Jer. 48:4,5,17; 50:46; 51:8; Ezek. 21:7;
26:15–18; 27:28–32; 27:35; 32:9,10,16; Jl. 2:1,6; Am. 8:7,8.

90 Jer. 50:13,23; 51:37,41,43,48; Ezek. 27:36; 32:10; Nah.
3:19.

91 Is. 5:17; Jer. 46:26; 49:19; Ezek. 29:13–16.

The world is full of death and destruction

92 Lev. 26:25,33; Is. 1:20; 10:4; 13:15,18; 15:9; 30:25; 31:8,9;

(166) "Hello I'm God & I'm here to help you"

34:2,5–7; 51:19; 63:3,6; 65:12; 66:16; Jer. 5:6; 6:21; 7:32; 9:16,22;
11:22; 12:12; 14:12,18; 15:2,3; 16:4; 19:6,10–12; 21:9; 24:10;
25:16,27,31; 27:8; 29:17,18; 34:17; 38:2; 42:16,17,22; 43:11;
44:12,13,27; 46:10,14; 47:6,7; 48:2,7,10,15; 49:14,26,37; 50:16,
21,27,30,35–37; 51:4,40,47,56; Ezek. 5:2,12,17; 6:3,7,11,12; 7:15;
11:5–12; 14:21; 21:9–23,28–32; 25:13; 26:6,8,11; 28:23; 29:8; 30:4–
6,11,17; 32:10–12,15; 33:27; 35:6,8; 39:23; Hos. 9:13; 11:6; 13:16;
Jl. 2:30; Am. 2:2; 4:10; 7:9; 8:3; Nah. 2:13; 3:1–4,15; Zeph. 2:12;
Zech. 13:8; Mt. 26:52; Lk. 21:24.

93 Dt. 28:26; Is. 5:25; 34:3; Jer. 7:33; 8:1,2; 16:4–8; 19:7;
25:33; 34:20; Am. 4:10; Zeph. 1:17.

94 Gen. 3:16; Ex. 22:24; Is. 3:25; 4:1; Jer 15:8.

95 Is. 5:24; 9:19; 34:9,10; Jer. 17:27; 32:29; 48:45; 49:27; 50:32;
51:30; Ezek. 5:4; 21:32; Hos. 8:14; Jl. 1:19,20; 2:30; Am. 1:4,7,10;
2:2,5; Nah. 1:6.

96 Is. 16:8–11; Jer. 50:16,26; Jl. 1:16.

97 1 Kg. 9:8; Is. 10:18,19; 17:1; 23:1; 24:10,12; Jer. 4:7,26; 9:11;
46:19; 48:8; 51:37; Ezek. 11:2–4; 21:17; 26:11,14; Mic. 3:12; 5:14;
Zeph. 1:15; 3:6; Mal. 1:4; Mt. 24:2; Mk. 13:2; Lk. 19:44; 21:6.

98 Is. 23:1–12.

99 Is 6:11; 14:22; 17:9; 24:6; 32:14; 33:8; 34:10; Jer. 4:7,25,29;
9:10,11; 22:6; 34:22; 44:2; 46:19; 48:9; 49:18; 50:3,13; 51:29,37,43;
Ezek. 26:19; 35:7,9; Am. 1:5,8; Zeph. 3:6.

100 Lev. 26:22,31,33–35,43; Dt. 29:23; 2 Kg. 22:19; Is. 1:7,8;
5:9; 6:11,12; 13:9; 15:6; 17:9; 24:1,12; 33:9; 34:11; 51:19; 59:7; Jer.
4:27; 6:8; 9:11; 12:10,11; 22:5; 44:2,6; 48:3,9,34; 50:3,13; 51:29;
Ezek. 5:14; 12:20; 15:8; 25:13; 26:5; 29:9,10,12; 30:12,14; 32:15;
33:28,29; 35:3,4,7,9; Hos. 5:8,9; 9:6; Jl. 2:3; 3:19; Mic. 6:13,16;
7:13; Zeph. 2:4,13,15; 3:6; Zech. 7:14; Mt. 23:38.

101 Lev. 26:31–33; Is. 6:11; 15:1; 23:1,13–15; 24:1,3; 34:10;
42:15; Jer. 4:7,20,23,26,29; 7:34; 9:10; 23:10; 25:11,12,38; 44:6;
46:19; 48:1,8; 49:3,13; 51:25,26,54; Ezek. 6:6,14; 12:20; 26:2,19,20;
29:9,10; 30:7; 33:27–29; 35:3,4; Am. 1:2; Jl. 1:10; Mic. 1:6; Nah.
1:4,5; Zeph. 1:13; 2:9; 3:6; Mal. 1:3.

102 Is. 7:23–25; 13:20–22; 14:23; 15:9; 17:2; 27:10; 32:14;
34:11,13–17; Jer. 9:11; 49:33; 50:39,40; 51:37; Ezek. 25:5,13;
29:8,11; 32:13,14; Zeph. 2:14,15.

103 Is. 16:1–4; 21:13–17; 24:1; Hos. 9:17.

The earth itself becomes an enemy
104 Gen 8:21,22; 9:9–17; Lk. 21:25.
105 Dt. 28:22; Is. 24:18; Am. 4:9; Hag. 2:17.

Bible references (167)

106 Dt. 11:17; 28:22,48; 2 Chr. 7:13; Is. 5:13; 42:15; 15:6; 19:5-9; 44:27; 50:2; Jer. 3:3; 14:3,4; 50:38; 51:36; Ezek. 30:12; Hos. 4:3; Jl. 1:20; Am. 4:7,8; 8:13; Nah. 1:4; Hag. 1:10; Zech. 14:17.

107 Gen 3:17-19; Lev. 26:19; Dt. 28:23.

108 Lev. 26:20; Dt. 11:17; 28:38-42; Is. 5:10; 24:7; 32:10,12,13; 33:9; Jer. 14:4; 48:33; Jl. 1:4,5,7,10-12; 2:4,5; Hag. 1:10,11.

109 Dt. 28:24; 29:23; Is. 51:6; Jer. 50:12; 51:43; Ezek. 26:4,14.

110 Lev. 26:26 Dt. 28:48; Is. 17:4; 51:19; Jer. 11:22; 14:12; 15:2; 16:4; 21:9; 24:10; 27:8; 29:17,18; 34:17; 38:2; 42:16,17,22; 44:12,13,27; Ezek. 5:12,16,17; 6:11,12; 7:15; 14:21; Hos. 8:7; 9:2; Jl. 1:17; Am. 4:6; Mt. 24:7; Mk. 13:8; Lk. 21:11.

111 Dt. 28:18; Jer. 14:5,6; 15:3; Ezek. 5:17; 14:21; 33:27; Jl. 1:18.

112 Is. 5:30; 13:10,13; 34:4; 50:3; 51:6; Jer. 4:23,28; Ezek. 32:7,8; Hos. 8:7; Jl. 2:2,10,30,31; 3:15,16; Am. 5:18,20; 8:9; Nah. 1:3; Hag. 2:21; Zeph. 1:15; Mt. 24:29; Mk. 13:24,25; Lk. 21:11,25,26.

113 Is. 51:15; Lk. 21:25.

114 Is. 5:25; 13:13; 24:1,18-20; Jer. 4:24; Jl. 2:10; 3:16; Mic. 1:4; Nah. 1:5,6; Hag. 2:21; Mt. 24:7; Mk. 13:8; Lk. 21:11.

115 Lev. 18:24,25,28; 20:22; Dt. 29:22; Is. 24:4-6; 26:21; Jer. 3:9; 4:28; 7:20; 16:18; 23:10; 25:13; 51:29; Ezek. 36:17.

People get desperate

116 Dt. 4:30; 2 Chr. 15:5,6; Jer. 4:20; 49:8,32; Ezek. 7:5,26; Mt. 24:8,21; Mk. 13:8,19; Lk. 21:22,23.

117 Is. 3:1-3; 9:21; Jer. 4:20,21; 51:57; Ezek. 30:4; Am. 5:13; Mic. 2:3.

118 Is. 3:6,7; Ezek. 30:13; Hos. 3:4; 8:10.

119 1 Kg. 9:7; 2 Chr. 7:20; 15:3; Is. 43:28; Jer. 7:12-14; 26:6; Ezek. 7:22,23; 24:21; Jl. 1:9,13.

120 Lev. 26:19; Is. 2:11-17; 5:15; 13:11; 23:9; 37:29; Jer. 13:9; Ezek. 21:26; Hos. 5:5; 7:10; Am. 6:8; Hab. 2:5; Zeph. 2:10.

121 Is. 47:8,9.

122 Is. 3:16-24; 22:12-14; 32:10-14; Hos. 12:8; Am. 6:4-7; Zeph. 1:18; Lk. 6:24,25.

123 Lev. 26:25; Num. 14:12; Dt. 28:21,22,48,59-61; 2 Chr. 7:13; 21:14,15; Is. 7:13-16,21-22; 8:21,22; Jer. 14:12,18; 15:2; 16:4; 21:6,9; 24:10; 27:8; 29:17,18; 34:17; 38:2; 42:17,22; 43:11; 44:13; Ezek. 5:12,17; 6:11,12; 7:15; 14:21; 28:23; 33:27; Hos. 12:9; Am. 4:10; 6:9,10; Zech. 8:10; 14:18; Lk. 21:11.

(168)   *"Hello I'm God & I'm here to help you"*

124 Is. 24:7–9,11; Jer. 7:34; 16:9; 25:10; 48:33; Ezek. 7:7; 26:13; Jl. 1:12,16.

125 Is. 3:26; 15:2–5,8; 16:7,11; 32:11,12; Jer. 4:8; 6:26; 7:29; 9:10,17–19; 14:1,2; 15:7; 30:5–7; 31:15; 46:12; 47:2,5; 48:31,32,34,36–38; 49:3; Ezek. 7:13,16–18; Hos. 4:3; Am. 5:16,17; 8:3,10; Mic. 1:8,16; Lk. 23:28.

126 Dt. 4:30; 2 Chr. 15:5; Is. 21:3,4; Jer. 12:12; 15:8; 46:5; 49:29; 50:34; 51:52; Ezek. 4:16,17; 12:18,19; 30:4,9,13,16; Mic. 4:9,10; Lk. 21:26.

127 Jer. 8:3; Hos. 10:8; Mk. 13:18; Lk. 23:29,30.

128 Dt. 28:34; Is. 13:12.

129 Is. 51:17,21; 63:3,6; Jer. 13:13; 25:15,16,27,28; Ob. 16; Nah. 3:11.

The world ends

130 Dt. 29:19; Jer. 49:12; Ezek. 21:3–5; 24:2–5; Mk. 9:49; Lk. 21:24; 23:31.

131 Lev. 26:44; Is. 6:13; 17:4–6; 24:13; 57:1; Jer. 4:27; 5:10,18; 21:9; 30:7,11; 38:2; 39:18; 44:14; 46:28; Ezek. 6:8; Jl. 2:32; Am. 3:12; 9:8; Ob. 17; Zech. 13:8; 14:2.

132 Ezek. 12:16; Am. 9:9; Lk. 21:18.

133 Mt. 24:22; Mk. 13:20.

134 Is. 65:8; Jer. 24:1–5; Ezek. 7:12; Am. 8:2; Mt. 24:14; Mk. 13:10; Lk. 21:9.

135 Lev. 26:45; Jer. 49:11; Zeph. 2:3.

136 Ex. 22:20; Dt. 7:10; 28:22,24,48,51; Is. 1:28; 10:22,23; 13:5,6,9; 14:23; 24:6; 28:2,22; 43:28; 51:6,19; Jer. 4:6; 11:23; 15:3; 24:10; 25:29; 34:18,19; 42:17; 44:7,27; 50:21,22; Ezek. 14:21; Hos. 7:13; 13:14; Jl. 1:15; Am. 1:8; 9:1; Nah. 1:8,9; Zeph. 1:2,3,18; 2:5; 3:8; Lk. 19:27.

137 Ex. 6:5; Lev. 26:9,42; Dt. 4:31; Jer. 33:14; Ezek. 16:60; Jn. 10:10.

IX   WHAT THE GOOD LIFE IS LIKE

I give you a new heart and my spirit

1 Dt. 30:6; Is. 57:15; Jer. 24:7; 32:39; Ezek. 11:19; 18:31; 36:26.

2 Ex. 31:3; Num. 11:17; 27:18; 2 Chr. 24:20; Is. 32:15; 42:1; 48:16; 57:15,16; 61:1; Ezek. 11:19; 36:27; 37:14; 39:29; Mic. 3:8; Hag. 2:5; Mt. 3:11; 12:28; 22:43; Mk. 1:8; 12:36; Lk. 3:16; 4:18; 24:49; Jn. 20:22.

3 Is. 11:2; 28:29; 30:21; 48:17; Jn. 3:8; 14:16,17,26; 15:26; 16:7–15.

4 Is. 42:16; 45:13; 50:7; Jer. 31:9; Ezek. 36:15; Jn. 8:14; 11:9; 14:4.

5 Is. 9:2; 10:17; 30:26; 42:16; Jn. 8:12; 11:9; 12:36,46.

6 Dt. 30:8; Is. 45:24; 58:8; Jer. 13:11; 32:40; Ezek. 18:9; 36:27; Mic. 3:8; Mal. 3:18.

7 Is. 59:21; Lk. 11:11–13.

You and I have a special relationship

8 Gen 18:19; Dt. 4:37; 7:6,7; 10:15; 14:2; 2 Chr. 6:6; Is. 14:1; 41:8,9; 42:1; 43:10,20; 44:1,2; 45:4; 49:7; 65:22; Ezek. 20:5; Hag. 2:23; Zech. 1:17; 2:12; 3:2; Lk. 9:35; Jn. 13:18; 15:16,19.

9 Is. 43:3,4; 44:2; Hos. 11:12; Am. 3:2; Zech. 2:8; 12:4.

10 Gen. 17:8; Ex. 6:7; 29:45,46; Lev. 11:44,49; 18:2; 19:2; 20:7; 22:33; 25:38; 26:12,45; Num. 10:10; 15:41; Dt. 10:17,21; 11:2; 27:9; 29:13; 30:7; Jg. 6:10; Is. 25:9; 41:10; 43:3; 45:15; 51:15,16,22; 55:5; 60:9; Jer. 7:23; 11:4; 19:3; 24:7; 27:21; 30:22; 31:1,18,23,33; 32:38; 33:4; 42:9,15; 50:18; Ezek. 11:20; 14:11; 34:24,30,31; 36:28; 37:23,27; Hos. 2:23; Am. 9:15; Zech. 8:8; 10:6; 13:9.

11 Ex. 19:5; 25:8; 29:46; Lev. 20:26; 26:11,12; Num. 5:3; 11:20; 35:34; Dt. 4:20; 7:21; 23:14; Is. 12:6; 41:8; 43:1; 54:5; 57:15; Hos. 2:19,20; 11:9; Jl. 3:21; Zeph. 3:15; Mal. 3:17; Jn. 14:23; 15:14,15; 17:6,9.

12 Dt. 14:1; Is. 65:23; Jer. 31:9,20; Hos. 1:10; 11:1; Mt. 5:9,45; 6:14,15; 11:27; 12:48–50; 16:27; 17:5; 20:23; 26:39,42; Mk. 3:33–35; 8:38; 9:7; Lk. 6:35; 8:21; 9:26,35; 10:22; 22:42; Jn. 3:16; 4:21,23; 5:17,19,20,23,36,37,43; 6:37,44,45,57,65; 8:18,19,28,35,54; 10:15,17,29,30,32,36; 11:41; 12:27,28,36; 14:2,7,9–12,20,28,31; 15:23,24; 16:15,26–28; 17:5,21,24,25; 18:11; 20:17.

13 2 Chr. 6:6; 7:14; Is. 4:3; 19:25; 34:16; 43:1,7; 45:3,4; 54:17; 57:13; 58:14; 62:2; 65:15; Jer. 25:29; Mal. 3:16; Jn. 6:27.

14 Ex. 20:6; Dt. 4:37; 5:10; 7:7,12,13; 10:15; 13:17; 23:5; 30:3; Is. 12:1; 14:1; 30:18,19; 43:4; 48:14; 49:10,13; 51:12; 52:9; 54:7,8,10; 55:7; 57:18; 60:10; 66:13; Jer. 30:18; 31:3,20; 33:26; Ezek. 39:25; Hos. 1:7; 2:23; 11:4; 14:4; Jl. 2:18; Am. 5:15; Zeph. 3:17; Zech. 1:16,17; 10:6; Mal. 1:2; Mt. 5:4,7; Jn. 5:20; 10:17; 14:21,23; 15:9; 16:27; 17:23.

15 Ex. 29:42,43; Dt. 4:30,31; 29:29; Is. 30:20; 50:4,5; Jer. 23:20; 30:24; 33:3; Ezek. 2:1; 3:22; Mt. 11:27; Lk. 10:22; Jn. 3:35; 8:31; 13:7,12–14; 16:12,15.

16 Ex. 6:7; 33:19; Dt. 4:35; 29:6; 1 Kg. 20:13,28; Is. 30:20; 49:23; 52:6; 60:16; Jer. 15:19; 22:16; Ezek. 16:62; 20:42,44;

28;24,26; 29:21; 34:27; 36:11; 37:6,14; 39:22; Hos. 2:20; Jl. 3:17; Zech. 4:14; 9:14; Mt. 5:8; Jn. 6:46; 14:19,21; 16:16,19,22; 17:25.
  17 Mt. 11:25–27; 13:11–17; 16:17: Mk. 4:11,12; Lk. 8:10; 10:21–24; Jn. 16:25.

I answer your prayers

  18 Dt. 4:29,36; 2 Kg. 22:19; 2 Chr. 7:14; 15:2,4; 34:27; Is. 30:19,20; 41:17; 49:8; 58:9; 65:24; Jer. 8:6; 29:12,13,14; 33:3; Ezek. 39:29; Hos. 14:8; Zech. 10:6; 13:9; Mal. 3:16; Mt. 6:8.
  19 Ex. 33:17; Mt. 7:7,8; 21:22; Mk. 11:24; Lk. 11:5–10; Jn. 14:13,14; 15:7,16; 16:23,24.
  20 Lk. 18:2–8.
  21 Mt. 7:7,8; 18:19; Lk. 11:9,10.
  22 Mt. 7:9–11.
  23 Mt. 9:29; 15:28; 17:20; 21:21,22; Mk. 9:23; 11:23; Lk. 17:6.

I take good care of you

  24 Dt. 4:31; 31:6; Jos. 1:5; Is. 41:17; 42:16; 44:21; 49:15,16; 62:12; Jer. 51:5; Zeph. 2:7; Jn. 8:29; 14:18.
  25 Ex. 3:12; 33:14; 34:10; Dt. 7:9; 10:21; 11:7; 20:1,4; 31:6; Jos. 1:5,9; 2 Chr. 15:2; 16:9; 20:17; Is. 12:5; 18:4; 25:10; 29:14; 41:10,13,14; 42:6; 43:5; 44:2; 45:1; 49:7,8; 50:7,8; Jer. 15:20; 30:11; 31:3; 42:11; 46:28; Ezek. 36:9; Am. 5:14; Mic. 7:15; Hag. 1:13; 2:4,5; Zech. 8:8; 10:5; Mt. 28:20; Jn. 8:29; 11:40; 16:32.
  26 Is. 4:6; 14:32; 28:16; 30:29: 31:5; 33:16; 49:2; 51:16; 52:12; 58:8,14; Hos. 14:7; Jl. 3:16; Nah. 1:7; Zech. 9:8,12,15; 12:8.
  27 Is. 41:10; 42:1; 43:2; 46:4; Hos. 14:8; Zech. 10:11.
  28 Is. 40:29–31.
  29 Ex. 20:20; 29:43,44; Lev. 20:8; 21:8,23; 22:9,16,32; Dt. 4:36; 11:2; Is. 1:25; 4:4; 48:10; Jer. 9:7; 31:18; Ezek. 20:12; 22:15; Zech. 13:9; Mal. 3:2,3; Jn. 15:2; 17:17.
  30 Dt. 2:7; 8:2–5; Jg. 2:21,22; Is. 30:20; 33:6; 48:21; Jer. 31:2,3; Ezek. 11:15,16; 20:10; Mt. 4:4; Lk. 4:4; 13:2–5; Jn. 9:3.
  31 Is. 40:11; 42:16; 48:17; 49:9,10; 57:18; 58:11; Jer. 30:8; 31:9,10; 50:19; Ezek. 34:11–16,22, 31; 37:24; Hos. 4:16; Mic. 2:12 Zeph. 3:13; Zech. 9:16; 10:3; Lk. 12:32; Jn. 10:1–16,26–29.

I make you strong

  32 Dt. 25:17,18; 1 Sam. 15:2; Is. 7:3–9; 9:1; 43:14; 49:17; 51:2 54:15; 66:5; Jer. 30:16,17,20; 33:24; Ezek. 28:24,26; 36:1–7; Mic. 4:11; Zeph. 2:6,7; 3:19; Zech. 12:9.
  33 2 Kg. 17:39; 19:32–34; 2 Chr. 20:15,17; Is. 37:33,34; Jer. 15:21; 31:11; 39:17; Mic. 4:10.

34 Is. 27:2–4.

35 Ex. 23:22; Dt. 30:7; 2 Kg. 19:34; Is. 37:35; 49:25.

36 Dt. 9:3; 31:3; Is. 30:27,28,30–33; 66:14.

37 Ex. 33:2; 34:11; Lev. 20:23; Dt. 6:19; 7:19; 11:23; 18:12; 20:4; Jos. 13:6; Jg. 6:9; 1 Sam. 15:2; Is. 27:1; 31:4; 35:4; 51:23; Jer. 2:3; 30:20; 51:36; Jl. 3:21; Zeph. 3:15,19; Mal. 3:11.

38 Ex. 23:27,28; Dt. 11:4; Is. 10:16; 41:11; 43:14,16,17; 49:26; 66:5; Ezek. 36:7; Zech. 9:5,6; 12:4.

39 Is. 17:13,14; Nah. 1:8.

40 Ex. 23:23; Dt. 7:20,23; 9:3; 12:29; 31:3,4; Is. 10:25,26; 18:5,6; Jer. 30:11,16; 45:28; Am. 2:9; Zech. 1:21.

41 Is. 25:10; Jl. 2:20; Mic. 4:12; Zeph. 3:18.

42 Dt. 11:8; Is. 12:2; 28:6; 29:22; 30:15; 41:10; 49:5; 60:21; Zech. 10:6,7,12; Zeph. 3:17; Lk. 10:18; Jn. 14:30.

43 Is. 41:15,16; 49:2; Jer. 15:20; Ezek. 3:8; Mic. 4:13; Zech. 9:13; 10:3,5.

44 Is. 11:4; 31:9; 49:2; Jer. 5:14; 23:29; Hos. 6:5; Zech. 12:6.

45 Dt. 7:24; 11:25; Jos. 1:5; 10:8; Mic. 3:8; Mt. 28:18; Lk. 10:19; Jn. 16:33; 17:2.

46 Is. 54:16,17.

47 Ex. 23:23,27,31; Lev. 26:7,8; Num. 21:34; Dt. 2:24, 31; 3:2; 4:38; 7:1,2,23,24; 11:23; 28:7; 31:5; Jos. 6:2,5; 8:1,18; 10:8; 11:6; Jg. 4:7; 1 Kg. 20:13–15,28; 1 Chr. 14:10,14,15; 2 Chr. 16:8; Jer. 15:20; Ezek. 25:14; Mic. 5:9; Mal. 4:3.

48 Ex. 23:27; Dt. 2:25; 7:23; 11:25; 28:10; Is. 19:16,17; 45:17; Jer. 33:9; Zech. 9:5.

49 Ex. 23:29,30; Dt. 7:22; 23:14; 31:3; 2 Chr. 17:10; Is. 29:5–8; 41:11,12; 50:9; 51:8; Jer. 49:1,2; Jl. 3:8; Mic. 5:9; Nah. 1:12,15; Zeph. 2:9.

I bless you

50 Dt. 30:3; Is. 61:7; Jer. 15:19; 29:14; 30:3,18; 31:18; 33:7,26; Ezek. 39:25; Zeph. 2:7; 3:20; Zech. 9:12.

51 Dt. 4:40; 5:16,29,33; 6:3,18; 12:25,28; 22:7; Is. 3:10; Jer. 7:23; 22:15,16.

52 Ex. 20:24; Num. 6:27; Dt. 7:13; 15:4,6; 28:2,8; Is. 30:18; 56:2; Jer. 17:7; Ezek. 37:26; Jl. 2:14; Hag. 2:19; Mt. 5:3–11; 11:6; 13:16; 25:34; Lk. 6:20–22; 7:23; 10:23; 11:28; Jn. 13:17; 20:29.

53 Dt. 7:14; 2 Chr. 25:9; Mal. 3:10; Mt. 19:29; Mk. 10:30; Lk. 6:38; 18:29,30.

54 Dt. 2:7; 14:29; 15:10,18; 23:20; 24:19; 28:8,12; 29:9; 30:5,9,16; Jos. 1:7,8; Is. 52:13; Ezek. 44:30.

55 Dt. 7:13; 16:15; 28:3–6,8,11; 30:9.

(172)   *"Hello I'm God & I'm here to help you"*

   56 Dt. 15:6; 28:12,13; Zech. 6:12.
   57 Num. 14:12; Dt. 9:14; 26:19; 28:1.
   58 Ex. 32:10; Lev. 26:9; Dt. 6:3; 7:13; 8:1; 11:21; 13:17; 30:5,16; Is. 44:3,4; 48:19; Jer. 3:16; 23:3; 30:19,20; 33:22; Ezek. 37:26; Hos. 1:10.

You're happy

   59 Is. 55:1; 58:11; Jer. 31:12,14,25; Mt. 5:6; Lk. 6:21; Jn. 4:13,14; 6:35,55; 7:37.
   60 Ex. 33:14; Is. 28:12; Jer. 6:16; Mt. 11:28,29; Jn. 14:27; 16:33; 20:19,21,26.
   61 Is. 30:26; 57:18,19; 58:8,11; 66:14; Jer. 30:17; 33:6; Hos. 6:1; 14:4; Mal. 4:2.
   62 Ex. 15:26; 23:25; Dt. 7:15.
   63 Is. 58:11; Jer. 31:12; Hos. 14:5–7; Jn. 7:38.
   64 Is. 4:2; 11:1; 27:6; 37:31; 61:11; Jer. 17:8; Ezek. 17:22–24.
   65 Dt. 16:15; Is. 9:1,3; 12:3; 30:19; 35:10; 51:11; 55:12; 60:20; 61:7; 66:14; Jer. 31:13; Mt. 5:4; Lk. 6:21; Jn. 15:11; 16:24; 17:13.
   66 Is. 9:3; 30:29; 35:10; 65:13,14; Zech. 10:7; Mal. 4:2; Lk. 6:21.
   67 Dt. 8:10; 10:21; Is. 12:1–6; 29:23; 41:16; 58:14; 61:10,11; 62:9; Jer. 31:7,23; Jl. 2:26; Zech. 10:7,12; Mal. 1:15.
   68 Jos. 5:9; Is. 54:4; 65:16; Ezek. 16:63; 39:26; Zeph. 3:11; Jn. 16:20–22.

You're good for the world

   69 Is. 43:7; 46:13; 49:3; 60:21; Jer. 13:11; Jn. 11:4; 13:31,32; 14:13; 15:8; 17:1,10.
   70 Is. 53:1,2; Mt. 4:19; Mk. 1:17; Lk. 5:4,10.
   71 1 Sam. 8:7; Mt. 10:40; Mk. 9:37; Lk. 9:48; 10:16; Jn. 13:20; 15:23; 17:10.
   72 Mt. 10:41,42; Mk. 9:41.
   73 Ezek. 3:24–27; 24:26,27; 29:21.
   74 Ex. 4:11,12,15; 19:3,6; Is. 51:16; Jer. 1:4; Mt. 10:19,20; Mk. 13:11; Lk. 12:11,12.
   75 Is. 54:17; Lk. 21:14,15.
   76 Is. 44:26; Zech. 6:15; Jn. 5:30–37; 8:17,18.
   77 Mt. 16:19; 18:18,20.
   78 Mt. 9:2,4–6; Mk. 2:5,8–11; Lk. 5:20,22–24; 7:41–48; Jn. 20:23.
   79 Is. 19:19–22; 56:3–5; 61:3; Jer. 12:14–17; 26:3.
   80 Is. 49:4; 53:10,11.

Bible references (173)

  81 Mt. 11:4,5; Mk. 16:17,18; Lk. 7:22; Jn. 9:39.
  82 Jn. 5:20; 14:12.
  83 Gen. 12:3; 18:18; 22:18; 26:4; 28:14; Jos. 1:6; Is. 19:24; 58:8,10; Jer. 4:2; Ezek. 34:26; Mic. 2:13; 5:7,8; Zech. 8:13; Mal. 4:6.
  84 Mt. 16:18.

You live forever
  85 Gen. 3:19,22; 6:3; Ex. 20:12; 23:26; Dt. 4:40; 5:16,33; 6:2; 11:9; 22:7; 25:15; 30:20; 32:47; Is. 14:21; 53:10; 65:22.
  86 Is. 51:14; Mt. 9:24; Mk. 5:39,41; Lk. 8:52,54; Jn. 11:11,25,26.
  87 Mt. 22:31,32; Mk. 12:26,27; Lk. 20:37,38.
  88 Hos. 6:2; Mt. 17:9,23; 20:19; 26:32; Mk. 9:31; 10:34; 14:28; Lk. 9:22; 18:33; 24:7,46; Jn. 2:19; 11:25,26.
  89 Mt. 20:23; Lk. 22:69; Jn. 3:13; 12:26; 14:2,3,12; 16:5,28; 17:11,13,24; 20:17.
  90 Mt. 22:29,30; Mk. 12:24,25; Lk. 20:34–38; 23:43.
  91 Lev. 18:5; Num. 21:8; Dt. 4:1; 5:33; 16:20; 30:6,16,19,20; Is. 55:3; Jer. 27:17; Ezek. 18:9,21,22,32; 20:11,13,21; 37:5,6,9,14; Hos. 6:2; Am. 5:4,6,14; Hab. 2:4; Zech. 10:9; Mal. 2:5; Mt. 18:8,9; 19:29; 25:46; Mk. 9:43,45; 10:30; Lk. 10:28; 18:30; 21:19; Jn. 3:15,16; 4:14; 5:24,40; 6:40,47,51,54,58; 8:35,51; 10:28; 12:25,50; 17:2,3.
  92 Is. 60:22; Hab. 2:3.

X WHAT HEAVEN ON EARTH WOULD BE LIKE

People praise my followers
  1 Is. 37:32; 60:1,2; Ezek. 20:41; 28:25.
  2 Is. 25:8; 29:22; 45:17; 49:23; 50:7; 54:4; Ezek. 34:29; 36:15; Jl. 2:19,26,27; Zeph. 3:18.
  3 Is. 9:1; 11:10; 43:4; 45:25; 49:5; 52:14,15; 55:5; 60:9; 62:3; 66:12; Jer. 30:19; 33:9; Mic. 7:16; Hag. 2:23; Zech. 6:13; 12:7; Jn. 8:28,50,54; 12:23,26; 13:31,32; 17:4,5,22.
  4 Dt. 4:5–8.
  5 Ex. 7:5; Dt. 28:10; Is. 45:24; 49:26; 60:14; 61:6,9; 62:2; 66:14; Jer. 33:9; Ezek. 36:36; 37:28; Zech. 12:5.
  6 Zech. 12:10–14.
  7 Dt. 26:19; Is. 22:23; 52:13; 53:12; 61:9; Mic. 5:4; Zeph. 3:19,20; Mal. 3:12.
  8 Is. 45:14; 55:5; 60:5,7,10,11,16; 61:5,6; 66:12.
  9 Is. 28:16; Mt. 21:42; Mk. 12:10,11; Lk. 20:17.

People turn to me
   10 Is. 2:2,3; Mic. 4:1,2.
   11 Is. 52:8; Jer. 31:6; 50:5; Zech. 2:6.
   12 Is. 11:15,16; 35:8; 49:11; 57:14.
   13 Is. 45:17; 51:6,8; 60:18; Jer. 23:6; 30:10; 33:16; 46:27; Zech. 13:1.
   14 Dt. 4:38; 30:3,4; Is. 10:21; 11:11,12; 27:12,13; 35:10; 41:9; 43:5,6; 46:3; 49:12,22,24,25; 51:11; 56:8; 60:4,8,9; Jer. 3:14,18; 16:14,15; 23:3,4,7,8; 24:6; 29:10,14; 30:10; 31:8,9,10,16,17,18; 32:37; 44:28; 46:27; 50:4; Ezek. 11:17; 20:34,41,42; 28:25; 34:13; 36:8,24; 37:12,14,21;n39:27,28; Hos. 1:11; 11:10,11; 12:6; 14:7; Jl. 3:7; Mic. 4:6,7; 5:3; 7:12; Zeph. 3:19,20; Zech. 8:6,7,8; 10:6,8,9,10; Mt. 24:31,40,41; Mk. 13:27; Lk. 17:34,35.
   15 Dt. 30:1; Ezek. 6:8–10; 14:22,23; Zech. 10:9.
   16 Is. 2:3; 66:20; Jer. 17:26; 50:4,5; Hos. 3:5; Mic. 4:1,2; 7:17; Zeph. 3:10; Zech. 8:20,21,22.
   17 Is. 11:10; 45:14,24; 49:7,23; 60:3,14; Jer. 15:19; Ezek. 16:61.
   18 Is. 14:1; 19:18; 55:5; Zech. 8:23.
   19 Is. 56:3,6–8; 66:21; Jer. 16:21; Zech. 2:11; 9:7; Ezek. 20:34.
   20 Ezek. 37:3–6,9,11–13.
   21 Is. 29:4; 45:13.
   22 Is. 18:7; 23:15–18; 60:7,13; Hag. 2:8; Zech. 14:14.
   23 Is. 10:22; Mic. 2:12.

Troublemakers are stopped
   24 Mt. 10:23; 24:39; Lk. 17:29,30; Jn. 14:3.
   25 Is. 11:12; 18:3; Mt. 16:27; 24:27,30; 25:31; 26:64; Mk. 8:38; 13:26; 14:62; Lk. 9:26; 17:24; 21:27.
   26 Is. 17:12,13; Zech. 1:21; 12:3; 14:2,5; Mt. 24:30; Lk. 21:20.
   27 Mt. 24:32,33; Mk. 13:28,29; Lk. 21:28–31.
   28 Is. 49:25: 52:10; Ezek. 38:–16; 39:7,8.
   29 Is. 59:19; Ezek. 38:17–23; 39:1–6; Jl. 2:21; Zech. 14:3–5,12–15.
   30 Zech. 9:14,15; 12:2,3,8.
   31 Is. 33:23; 45:24; Ezek. 39:9,10; Mic. 7:16,17.
   32 Ex. 34:24; Is. 11:13; 14:2; 30:25; 32:19; 33:23; 49:17,25; 60:12; Ezek. 28:26; 39:17–20; Zeph. 1:7,8; Zech. 12:9.
   33 Is. 66:24; Ezek. 39:11–16; Mk. 9:48.
   34 Is. 40:1,2.

Bad things have to go
   35 Is. 2:4; 66:16; Jer. 25:31; 49:38; Ezek. 20:35,36; Jl.

Bible references (175)

3:2,11,12,14; Mic. 4:3; Zeph. 3:8; Mt. 12:36,37; 16:27; 19:28; Lk. 22:30; Jn. 5:22,27,29; 12:31,48.

36 Is. 27:12; Jer. 15:7; Ezek. 20:37; 34:17; Hos. 6:11; Mt. 3:11,12; 13:47–50; 25:32,33; Lk. 3:16,17.

37 Mt. 13:24–30,37–40.

38 Is. 26:19; 57:16; Mt. 25:34; Lk. 14:14; Jn. 5:21,25,28,29; 6:39,40,44,54; 11:25.

39 Ezek. 20:38; Mt. 13:41; 25:41; Jn. 12:31.

40 Mt. 7:21–23; 22:11–14.

41 Ezek. 34:17–22.

42 Zeph. 3:11,12.

43 Is. 35:8; 52:1; Jl. 3:17; Zech. 9:7; 14:21.

44 Lev. 26:30; Jg. 2:3; 10:11–14; Is. 2:9,18,20,21; 17:8,10,11; 19:1; 21:9; 28:18; 41:5,6; 42:17; 45:16; 46:1,2; 57:11–13; Jer. 2:26–28; 10:11; 11:12,13; 19:13; 22:20,22; 43:12,13; 46:25; 48:7,13,46; 49:3; 50:1,2,6; 51:44,47,52; Ezek. 6:3–6,13; 7:24; 14:3–5; 20:3,31; 30:13; 37:23; Hos. 2:16,17; 4:17–19; 8:5; 10:2,5–8; 12:11; Am. 3:14; 5:5; 7:9; Mic. 1:7; 5:13,14; Nah. 1:14; Hab. 2:19; Zeph. 1:4,5; 2:11; Zech. 13:2; Lk. 16:15.

45 Is. 9:14,15; 25:7; 28:17; 29:14; 44:25; Jer. 8:12; 14:15,16; 20:4,6; 23:12,15,30–32,34,39,40; 27:15; 28:16; 29:15,16,21,22,25–28,31,32; Ezek. 13:3,8–15; 14:9,10; 22:28; 44:12; Hos. 4:4–10; 7:13; Mic. 3:6; 7:4; Zech. 13:2–6; Mal. 1:10; 2:1–4,9; Mt. 23:13–16,23,25,27,29,33; Mk. 12:40; Lk. 9:62; 11:42–44,46,52; 20:47.

46 Is. 8:19,20; 24:23; 44:25; 47:12–15; Jer. 50:36; Ezek. 13:17–23; Mic. 3:6,7; 5:12; Mal. 3:5.

47 Jer. 50:20.

People do what's good

48 Is. 14:32; 41:20; 62:1; 66:7–9; Jer. 30:20; Mt. 5:3,10,12; 16:19,28; 19:14,21; Mk. 9:1,47; 10:14,21; Lk. 6:20,23; 9:27; 12:32; 17:20,21; 18:16,22; 22:29.

49 Is. 42:9; 43:18,19; 48:6,7; 65:17; 66:22; Mt. 19:28.

50 Is. 2:2,11,17; 17:7; 33:5,10; 59:19; 66:23; Jer. 3:17; 30:9; Ezek. 20:40; 34:24; Zeph. 3:9; Zech. 14:9, 16; Mal. 1:11,14.

51 Is. 24:23; 33:22; 40:10; 43:15; 44:5,6; 45:23; 51:5; 66:18; Jer. 3:16,17; Ezek. 20:33; 37:22; Ob. 21; Mic. 2:13; 4:7; Zeph. 2:11; 3:15; Zech. 9:10; 14:9,16,17; Mal. 1:14; Jn. 12:32.

52 Ex. 29:45; Num. 14:21; Dt. 4:32–36; Is. 4:5; 33:17; 35:2; 40:5,10; 52:8; 66:18; Ezek. 37:26,27; 39:21; 43:7,9; Jl. 2:27; 3:17; Zeph. 3:17, Zech. 2:10–12; 8:3; 14:5; Mal. 3:1.

53 Is. 44:3; Jl. 2:28,29.

54 Is. 11:9; 33:6; 54:13; Jer. 31:31–34; Hab. 2:14.

55 Is. 29:18,20,24; 32:3–7; 35:5.
56 Mt. 5:19; 11:11; 18:4; Lk. 7:28.
57 Is. 1:26; 4:3; 28:6,17; 32:16,17; 33:5; 35:9; 48:18; 54:14; 60:17,21; 65:16; Jer. 31:23,40; 33:16; Jl. 3:17; Am. 5:24; Zech. 8:3; 14:20,21.
58 2 Sam. 7:4–16; 1 Kg. 9:5; 1 Chr. 17:3–14; 22:8–10; 28:3,6,7; 2 Chr. 7:18; Is. 9:6,7; 16:5; 22:20–24; 32:1,2; Jer. 3:15; 17:25; 22:4; 23:4–6; 30:9,21; 33:17,18; Ezek. 29:21; 34:23,24; 37:24,25; Hos. 1:11; Am. 9:11,12; Ob. 21; Mic. 5:2,4; Zech. 3:7; 6:13; 10:4; Mt. 19:28.
59 1 Sam. 2:35; Is. 9:6; 22:22; Jer. 30:9.

The world is peaceful
60 Lev. 26:6; 2 Sam. 7:10; 2 Kg. 21:8; 1 Chr. 17:9; Is. 9:7; 32:17,18; 48:18; 54:10; 55:12; 57:19; 60:17,21; Jer. 24:6; 31:27,28,40; 32:41; 42:10; Ezek. 34:25; 37:26; Am. 9:15; Mic. 5:5; Zech. 8:12; 9:10; Mal. 2:5.
61 Ex. 34:24; 2 Sam. 7:10; 1 Chr. 17:9; Is. 14:4; 16:4; 33:19; 49:19; 54:14; 60:18; Jer. 31:22; Nah. 1:15; Zech. 2:4,5; 9:8; 14:11.
62 Lev. 26:6; Is. 2:4; 9:5; 16:4; 19:23–25; 33:21; Hos. 1:11; 2:18; Mic. 4:3,4; Zech. 9:10.
63 Lev. 26:6; Is. 35:9; 43:10; Ezek. 34:25,28; Hos. 2:18.
64 Is. 11:6–9; 65:25.
65 Is. 33:18; Ezek. 28:24.
66 Lev. 25:18,19; 26:5,6; Dt. 12:10; 25:19; Jos. 1:12,13; 2 Sam. 7:11; Is. 14:3,4,7; 32:17,18; 54:14; Jer. 23:4,6; 30:10; 32:37; 33:6,16; 46:27; 50:34; Ezek. 28:26; 34:27,28; 39:26; Hos. 2:18; Mic. 5:4; Zeph. 3:13,15; Zech. 3:10; 14:11.
67 Is. 33:20; 54:15.

The earth is fruitful again
68 Ex. 34:24; Lev. 26:42; Num. 34:2; Dt. 4:38; 6:18; 7:1; 11:8,24; 12:10,20; 15:4; 16:20; 20:16; 25:19; 30:16; 32:47; Jos. 1:3,4; 2 Chr. 7:14; Is. 33:17; 51:3; 60:15; 62:4; 65:9; 66:13; Jer. 3:18; 33:11; Ezek. 36:12; 47:14; Jl. 2:24,25; Am. 9:12; Mt. 5:5.
69 Lev. 26:4; Dt. 11:14; 28:12; Is. 30:23; Jer. 5:24; Ezek. 34:26; Jl. 2:23; Zech. 8:12; 10:1.
70 Is. 29:17; 30:25; 32:15; 35:1,2,6,7; 41:18,19; 43:19,20; 44:3; 51:3; 55:13; 65:10; Zech. 14:10.
71 Is. 33:21; Ezek. 47:8–12; Zech. 14:8.
72 Is. 60:5; Jer. 5:22.
73 Is. 49:10; Zech. 14:6.
74 Is. 60:19,20; Zech. 14:7.

Bible references

75 Lev. 25:19; 26:4,5,10; Dt. 11:15; Jos. 24:13; Is. 30:23; 32:20; 37:30; 62:8,9; 65:21–23; Jer. 31:5; 32:14,15,43,44; Ezek. 28:26; 34:27; 36:8,9,34,35; Hos. 2:21–23; Jl. 2:22,24; Am. 9:13,14; Hag. 2:15–19; Zech. 8:12; Mal. 3:11.

76 Ex. 16:4,12; 23:25; Lev. 25:19; 26:5; Num. 21:16; Dt. 8:9,10; 11:15; Is. 1:19; 33:16; 49:10; 51:14; 65:13; Ezek. 34:29; 36:29,30; Jl. 2:19,26; Mal. 3:11.

77 Is. 30:23,24; 32:20; Jer. 31:24; 33:12,13.

78 Ex. 3:8,17; 6:4,8; 33:1–3; Lev. 20:24; 25:38; Num. 14:24; 15:2,18; 33:53; Dt. 1:8,36; 4:1,40; 5:16; 6:3,18,19; 8:1,7–10; 9:23; 11:9–12,21,29,31; 12:10; 15:4; 16:20; 18:9; 27:2,3; 28:8,11; 30:5,20; Jos. 1:2, 13; Jg. 1:2; 2:1; 6:9; 2 Sam. 7:10; 1 Chr. 17:9; Is. 14:1; 57:13; 60:21; Jer. 7:3,7; 11:5; 23:8; 25:5; 27:11; 30:3; Ezek. 11:17; 20:6,15,42; 28:25; 34:13; 36:12,28; 37:25; Jl. 3:18; Am. 2:10; 9:13; Ob. 17; Zech. 8:12; Mal. 3:12.

79 Is. 25:6; Jer. 31:14; Mt. 8:11; 26:29; Mk. 14:25; Lk. 13:29; 22:15–18,29,30.

Everyone is happy and prosperous

80 Dt. 15:4; Is. 54:13; 60:5–7; 65:22; Jer. 31:23; 32:44; 33:6; 48:47; 49:6,39; 50:19; Ezek. 16:53–55; Jl. 3:1; Am. 9:14; Mic. 4:8; Nah. 2:2; Hag. 2:9; Zech. 1:17.

81 Dt. 20:16; Jos. 24:13; Is. 44:26,28; 49:17,18; 58:12; 61:4; 65:21; Jer. 30:18; 31:4,38,39; 33:7; Ezek. 28:26; 36:10,11,33,35,37,38; Am. 9:11,14; Mic. 7:11; Zech. 12:6; 14:11.

82 Is. 28:5; 54:11,12; 60:17.

83 Is. 66:10–12.

84 Is. 14:7; 25:8; 29:19; 32:20; 35:6; 49:13; 51:3; 55:12; 60:5; 65:18,19; Jer. 30:19; 31:4,13; Hos. 1:11; Zech. 8:18,19; 9:16; Mt. 13:43.

85 Is. 24:14–16; 29:19; 60:6,18; Jer. 31:12; 33:10,11; Mt. 21:16.

86 Is. 62:4,5; 65:19.

87 Is. 33:24; Zech. 9:17.

88 Ex. 23:26; Dt. 7:14; Is. 54:1–3.

89 Is. 25:8; 65:20,23; Ezek. 36:12–14.

90 Dt. 10:22; Is. 9:3; 29:23; 49:19–21; 60:22; Ezek. 36:10,11; Zech. 8:4,5; 10:8.

91 Gen. 8:21; Is. 66:22; Jer. 17:25; 31:36,37; 33:20,21,25,26; Ezek. 37:25; Jl. 3:20.

XI IT'S UP TO YOU!

1 Dt. 11:26–28; 30:1; Jer. 21:8.
2 Lk. 14:28–32.

3 Hos. 14:9; Mic. 6:9; Mt. 7:24–27; Lk. 6:46–49.
4 Is. 43:8; 55:2,6; Hos. 10:12; Mic. 6:8; Mt. 3:2; 4:17; Mk. 1:15; Jn. 12:35,36; 15:22,24.
5 Gen. 17:9–14; Lev. 12:3; Jos. 5:2; Is. 28:22: 33:13; 43:26; 44:21; 46:8,9; 52:2; 62:6; Jer. 4:3,4; Hos. 10:12; Mal. 4:4.
6 Dt. 10:16; Is. 50:5; Ezek. 2:8; Zech. 1:4–6.
7 Num. 11:23; Is. 50:2; 59:1; Jer. 4:14; 13:27; Hos. 8:5.
8 Is. 1:5; 28:22; 48:16; 51:22; 55:1,3; Jer. 4:1; 27:12,13,17; 31:22; 50:34; Ezek. 18:31; 33:11; Hos. 2:14,15; Zech. 2:7; Mt. 11:28; Jn. 6:35,37; 7:37.
9 Mt. 22:2–10; Lk. 14:16–24.
10 Mt. 8:22; Lk. 9:60.
11 Dt. 29:10–15; 30:15,19; Jos. 24:14,15.

Bibliography

The Amplified Bible, 8th ed. Grand Rapids, Mich.: Zondervan Publishing House, 1971.

Beck, William F. *The New Testament in the Language of Today*, 5th ed. St. Louis, Mo.: Concordia Publishing House, 1964.

The King James Version of The Holy Bible. New York: Harper and Row.

The Living Bible Paraphrased. Wheaton, Ill.: Tyndale House Publishers, 1971.

The Good News Bible, Today's English Version.: New York: Thomas Nelson, Inc., under license from The American Bible Society, 1976.

The Oxford Annotated Bible; The Revised Standard Version of the Holy Bible. New York; Oxford University Press, 1962.

Oxford Study Edition: *The New English Bible with the Apocrypha*. New York: Oxford University Press, 1976.

Phillips, J. B. *The New Testament in Modern English for Schools*, 3rd ed. London: Geoffrey Bles, Ltd., 1960.

The Revised Standard Version of the Holy Bible. New York: Thomas Nelson and Sons, 1952.

Text Edition. *New American Standard Bible New Testament*. La Habra, Cal.: The Lockman Foundation, 1963.

Williams, Charles B. *The New Testament in the Language of the People*. Chicago: Moody Press, 1963.